George Buchanan, Thomas Maitland

De Jure Regni apud Scotos

Or, A Dialogue concerning the due Priviledge of Government in the Kingdom of Scotland

George Buchanan, Thomas Maitland

De Jure Regni apud Scotos
Or, A Dialogue concerning the due Priviledge of Government in the Kingdom of Scotland

ISBN/EAN: 9783337147402

Printed in Europe, USA, Canada, Australia, Japan

Cover: Foto ©ninafisch / pixelio.de

More available books at **www.hansebooks.com**

DE Jure Regni APUD SCOTOS

OR, A DIALOGUE,

Concerning the due Priviledge of GOVERNMENT In the Kingdom of SCOTLAND.

BETWIXT
GEORGE BUCHANAN
And
THOMAS MAITLAND,
By the said
GEORGE BUCHANAN.
Translated out of the Original *Latine* into *English*.
By PHILALETHES.

LONDON, Printed for Richard Baldwin. 1689.

A
DIALOGUE

Treating of the

JUS, or RIGHT,

Which the KINGS of *Scotland* have for exercising their Royal Power.

George Buchanan, AUTHOR.

George Buchanan to King *James*, the sixth of that name King of *Scots*, wisheth all health and happiness.

I Wrote *several years ago, when amongst us affairs were very turbulent, a Dialogue of the right of the Scots Kings, wherein I endeavoured to explain from the very beginning (if I may so say) what right, or what authority both Kings and People have one with another. Which Book, when for that time it seemed somewhat profitable, as shutting the mouths of some, who more by importunate clamours at that time, than what was right, inveighed against the course of affairs, requiring they might be levelled according to the rule of right reason; but matters being somewhat more peaceable, I also having laid down my Arms, very willingly devoted my self to publick concord. Now having lately fallen upon that disputation, which I found amongst my Papers, and perceiving therein many things which might be necessary for your Age (especially you being placed in that part of humane affairs) I thought*

The Epistle Dedicatory to the KING.

good to publish it, that it might be a standing witness of mine affection towards you, and admonish you of your duty towards your Subjects. Now many things perswaded me that this my endeavour should not be in vain: Especially your Age not yet corrupted by prave opinions, and inclination far above your Years for undertaking all Heroical and noble attempts, spontaneously making haste thereunto, and not only your promptitude in obeying your Instructors and Governours, but all such as give you sound admonition, and your Judgment and Diligence in examining Affairs, so that no mans Authority can have much weight with you, unless it be confirmed by probable reason. I do perceive also, that you by a certain natural instinct do so much abhor flattery, which is the Nurse of Tyranny, and a most grievous plague of a Kingdom, so as you do hate the Court Solecisms and Barbarisms no less, than those that seem to censure all elegancy, do love and effect such things, and every where in discourse spread abroad, as the Sawce thereof, these Titles of Majesty, Highness, and many other unsavoury compellations. Now albeit your good natural diposition, and sound instructions, wherein you have been principled, may at present draw you away from falling into this Error, yet I am forced to be somewhat jealous of you, lest bad company, the fawning foster-mother of all vices, draw aside your soft and tender mind into the worst part; especially seeing I am not ignorant, how easily our other senses yeild to seduction. This Book therefore I have sent unto you to be not only your monitor, but also an importunate and bold Exactor, which in this your tender and flexible years may conduct you in safety from the rocks of flattery, and not only may admonish you, but also keep you in the way you are once entred into: And if at any time you deviate, it may reprehend and draw you back, the which if you obey, you shall for your self and for all your Subjects acquire Tranquility and Peace in this life, and Eternal Glory in the Life to come. Farewel, from Stirveling, the Tenth day of January in the Year of Mans Salvation one Thousand Five Hundred Seventy Nine.

A DIA-

THE TRANSLATOR TO THE READER.

Candid Reader,

I Have presumed to trouble your attention with the Ceremony of a Preface, the end and design of which is not to usher in my Translation to the World with curious embellishments of Oratory (that serving only to gratifie, or enchaunt a Luxuriant fancy) but allennarly to Apologize for it, in case a *Zoilus*, or a *Momus*, shall happen to peruse the same. Briefly, then I reduce all that either of these will (as I humbly perceive) object against this my work, to these two Generals, *Prevarication* and *Ignorance*. First, they will call me a prevaricator or prevaricating Interpreter, and that upon two accounts. First, Because I have (say they) sophisticated the genuine sence and meaning of the learned Author, by interpreting and foisting in spurious words of mine own. Secondly, That I have quite alienated the literal sence in other places by a too Paraphrastical exposition. To the first I answer, that none are ignorant, that the Original of this piece is a Lofty *Laconick* stile of Latin: Now I once having undertaken *Provinciam Interpretis*, behoved to render my interpretation somewhat plain and obvious, which I could never do in some places, without adding some words (*Claritatis gratiâ*) but always I sought out the scope (as far as my shallow capacity could reach) and suited them thereunto. Wherein I am hopeful, that no ingenuous impartial Reader not prepossessed with prejudice against the matter contained in the Original, and consequently against the Translation thereof, will find much matter of quarrel upon that account, if he will but take an overly view of the Original,

and

and so compare the Translation therewith. For I have been very sparing in adding ought of my own. To the second branch of the first Challenge I answer briefly; there are none who have the least smattering of common sence, but know well enough, that it is *morally impossible* for an Interpreter to make good Language of any Latine piece, if he shall alwayes *verbum verbo reddere*; I mean, if he adhere so close to the very rigour of the Original, as to think it illicite to use any *Paraphrase*, although the succinctness and summary comprehensiveness of the Original Stile even cry aloud for it, as it were; but to silence in a word these Critical Snarlers, where ever I have used any *Paraphrase*, I likewise have set down the exposition *ad verbum* (to the best of my knowledge) as near as I could.

The Second Challenge is of *Ignorance*, and that because I have passed by some Latine verses of *Seneca*, which are at the end of this *Dialogue*, containing the Stoicks description of a King, without Translating them into English: Now, true it is, I have done so, not because I knew not how to interpret them (for I hope, Candid Readers at least will not so judge of me) but because I thought it not requisite to meddle with them, unless I could have put as specious a lustre upon them, as my Pen would have pulled off them (for otherwise I would have greatly injured them) which could never be done without a sublime Vein of Poesie, wherein I ingenuously profess ignorance: so that if the last Challenge be thus understood, *transeat* because

Nec fonte labra prolui Cabalino,
Nec in bicipiti somniasse Parnasso,
Memini, ut repente sic Poeta prodirem.

And hence it is, that all the Latin Verses, which occur in this *Dialogue*, are by me Translated into Prose, as the rest: But I fear I have wearied your Patience too long already, and therefore I will go no further, I wish you satisfaction in the Book, and so

Vive & Vale.

A DIALOGUE

Concerning that

JUS or RIGHT

OF

GOVERNMENT

Amongſt the

SCOTS.

PERSONS

GEORGE BUCHANAN
And
THOMAS MAITLAND.

Thomas Maitland being of late returned home from *France*, and I ſeriouſly enquiring of him the ſtate of Affairs there, began (for the love I bear to him) to exhort him to continue in that courſe he had taken to honour, and to entertain that excellent hope in the progreſs of his Studies. For if I, being but of an ordinary ſpirit, and almoſt of no fortune, in an illiterate Age, have ſo wreſtled with the iniquity of the times, as that I ſeem to have done ſomewhat: then certainly they who are born in a more happy Age, and who have maturity of Years, Wealth and Pregnancy of Spirit, ought not to be deterred by pains from noble deſigns, nor can ſuch deſpair being aſſiſted by ſo many helps. They ſhould therefore go on with vigour to illuſtrate learning, and to commend themſelves and thoſe of their Nation to the memory of after Ages and poſterity. Yea if they would but beſtir themſelves herein ſomewhat actively, it might come to paſs, that they would eradicate out of Mens minds that opinion, that Men in the cold regions of the World, are at as great distance from Learning, Humanity and all Endowments of the Mind, as they are distant from the Sun. For as Nature hath granted to the *Africans, Egyptians*, and many other Nations more subtile motions of the Mind, and a greater sharpness of Wit, yet she hath not altogether so far cast off any Nation, as to shut up from it an entry to Vertue and Honour. Hereupon, whilst he did speak meanly of of himself (which is his modesty) but of me more affectionatly than truely: at last the tract of discourse drew us on so far, that when he had asked me concerning the troubled state of our Country, and I had answered him as far as I judged convenient for that time; I began by course to ask him, what was the opinion of the *French*'s or other Nations with whom he had conversed in *France*, concerning our Affairs? For I did not question, but that the novelty of Affairs (as is usual) would give occasion and matter of discourse thereof to all. Why (saith he) do you desire that of me? For seeing you are well acquainted with the course of Affairs, and is not ignorant what the most part of men do speak, and what they think. You may easily guess in your own Conscience, what is, or at least should be the Opinion of all. B. But, the further that foreign Nations are at a distance, they have the less causes of Wrath, Hatred, Love and other Perturbations, which may divert the Mind from Truth, and for the most part they so much the more judge of things sincerely, and freely speak out what they think: that very freedom of speaking and conferring the thoughts of the Heart doth draw forth many obscure things, discovers intricacies, confirms doubts and may stop the Mouth of wicked men, and teach such as are weak. M. Shall I be ingenuous with you? B. Why not? M. Although I had a great desire after so long a time, to visit my native Country, Parents, Relations and Friends, yet nothing did so much inflame my desire, as the clamour of a rude multitude: For albeit I thought my self well enough fortified either by my own constant Practice, or the moral precepts of the most Learned, yet when I came to fall upon the present case, I know not how I could conceal my Pusilanimity. For when that horrid villany not long since here perpetrated, all with one voice did abominate it, the Author hereof not being known; the multitude, which is more acted by precipitancy, than ruled by deliberation, did charge the fault of some few upon all; and the common hatred of a particular crime did redound to the whole Nation, so that even such as were most remote from any suspicion were inflamed with the infamy of other mens crimes. When therefore this storm of calumny was calmed, I betook my self very willingly into this port, wherein notwithstanding I am afraid, I may dash upon a Rock. B. Why, I pray you? M. Because the atrociousness of

that

that late crime doth seem so much to inflame the Minds of all already exasperated, that now no place of Apology is left. For, how shall I be able to sustain the impetuous assaults, not only of the weaker sort, but also of those who seem to be more sagacious, who will exclaim against us, that we were content with the slaughter of an harmless Youth, an unheard of cruelty, unless we should shew another new example of atrocious cruelty against Women, which sex very Enemies do spare when Cities are taken by force. Now from what villany will any dignity or Majesty deter those, who thus rage against Kings? or what place for mercy will they leave, whom neither the weakness of Sex, nor innocency of Age will restrain? Equity, Custom, Laws, the respect to Soveraignty Reverence of lawful Magistracy, which henceforth they will either retain for shame, or coerce for fear, when the power of supream Authority is exposed to the ludibry of the basest of the People, the difference of equity and miquity, of honesty and dishonesty being once taken away, almost by a publick consent, there is a degeneracy into cruel barbarity. I know I shall hear these and more atrocious then these spoken so soon as I shall return into *France* again; all mens Ears in the mean time being shut from admitting any Apology or satisfaction. *B.* But I shall easily liberate you of this fear, and our Nation from that false crime. For, if they do so much detest the atrociousness of the first crime, how can they rationally reprehend severity in revenging it? or if they take it ill, that the Queen is taken order with, they must needs approve the first deed; choose you then, which of the two would you have to seem cruel. For neither they nor you can praise or reproach both, provided you understand your selves. *M.* I do indeed abhor and detest the Kings Murther, and am glad that the Nation is free of that guilt, and that it is charged upon the wickedness of some few. But this last fact I can neither allow or disallow; for it seems to me a famous and memorable deed, that by counsel and diligence they have searched out that Villany, which since the Memory of Man is the most hainous, and do pursue the perpetrators in a hostile manner. But in that they have taken order with the chief Magistrate, and put contempt upon Soveraignty, which amongst all Nations hath been always accounted great and sacred. I know not how all the Nations of *Europe* will relish it, especially such as live under Kingly Government; surely the Greatness and Novelty of the fact doth put me to a demur, albeit I am not ignorant what may be pretended on the contrary, and so much the rather, because some of the Actors are of my intimate Acquaintance. *B.* Now I almost perceive, that it doth perhaps not trouble you so much, as those of forreign Nations, who would be judges of the Vertues of others to whom

you

you think satisfaction must be given. Of these I shall set down three sorts especially, who will vehemently enveigh against that deed. The first kind is most pernicious, wherein those are, who have mancipated themselves to the lusts of Tyrants, and think every thing just and lawful for them to do, wherein they may gratifie Kings, and measure every thing not as it is in it self, but by the lust of their Masters. Such have so devoted themselves to the lusts of others, that they have left to themselves no liberty either to speak or do. Out of this Crew have proceeded those, who have most cruelly Murthered that Innocent Youth, without any cause of Enmity, but through hope of gain, Honour and Power at Court to satisfie the lust of others. Now whilst such feign to be sorry for the Queens case, they are not grieved for Her misfortunes, but look for their own security, and take very ill to have the reward of their most Hainous Crime, (which by hope they swallowed down) to be pulled out of their Throat. I judge therefore that this kind of Men should not be satisfied so much by reasoning, as chastised by the severity of Laws, and force of Arms. Others again are all for themselves; these Men, though otherwise not Malicious, are not grieved for the publick Calamity (as they would seem to be) but for their own Domestick damages, and therefore they seem to stand in need rather of some comfort, than of the remedies of perswasive reasoning and Laws. The rest is the rude multitude, which doth admire at all Novelties, reprehend many things, and think nothing is right, but what they themselves do or see done: For how much any thing done doth decline from an Ancient Custome, so far they think it is fallen from Justice and Equity. And because these be not led by Malice and Envy, nor yet by Self-interest, the most part will admit Information, and to be weaned from their Error, so that being convinced by the strength of reason, they yield: Which in the matter of Religion, we find by experience very often in these days, and have also found it in preceding Ages. There is almost no man so wild, that cannot be tamed, if he will but patiently hearken to instruction.

M. Surely we have found oftentimes that very true. *B.* When you therefore deal with this kind of people so clamorous and very importunate, ask some of them, what they think concerning the punishment of *Caligula, Nero* or *Domitian,* I think there will be none of them so addicted to the name *King,* that will not confess, they were justly punished. *M.* Perhaps you say right, but these very same men will forthwith cry out, that they complain not of the punishment of Tyrants, but are grieved at the sad Calamities of Lawful Kings. *B.* Do you not then perceive how easily the People may be pacified? *M.* Not indeed, unless you say some other thing. *B.* But I shall cause you understand it in few words, the People (you say) approve the Murther of Tyrants, but compassionate the misfortune of Kings, would they not then change their Opinion, if they clearly understood what the difference is betwixt a Tyrant and a King? do you not think that this might come to pass, as in many other cases? *M.* If all would confess that Tyrants are justly killed, we might have a large entry made open to us for the rest, but I find some men, and these not of small Authority, who while they make Kings liable to the penalties of the Laws, yet they will maintain Tyrants to be Sacred persons; but certainly by a preposterous judgment, if I be not mistaken, yet they are ready to maintain their Government, albeit immoderate and intolerable, as if they were to Fight for things both Sacred and Civil. *B.* I have also met with several persons oftentimes, who maintain the same very pertinaciously; but whether that opinion be right or not, we shall further discuss it hereafter at better conveniency. In the mean time, if you please, let us conclude upon this, upon condition, that unless hereafter it be not sufficiently confirmed unto you, you may have liberty to retract the same. *M.* On these terms indeed I will not refuse it. *B.* Let us then conclude these two to be contraries, a *King* and a *Tyrant*. *M.* Be it so. *B.* He therefore that shall explain the Original and Cause of Creating Kings, and what the duties of Kings are towards their People, and of People towards their Kings, will he not seem to have almost explained on the other hand, what doth pertain to the nature of a Tyrant. *M.* I think so. *B.* The representation then of both being laid out, do you not think that the People will understand also, what their duty is towards both? *M.* It is very like they will. *B.* Now contrariwise, in things that are very unlike to one another, which yet are contained under the same *Genus*, there may be some similitudes, which may easily induce imprudent Persons into an Error. *M.* Doubtless, there may be such, and especially in the same kind, where that which is the worst of the two doth easily personate the best of both, and studies nothing more, than to impose the same upon such as are ignorant. *But.* Have you not some representation of a King and of a Tyrant impressed in your mind? For if you have it, you will save me much pains. *M.* Indeed I could easily express what *Idea* I have of both in my mind, but I fear, it may be rude and without form, therefore, I rather desire to hear what your opinion is, lest whilst you are a refuting me, our discourse become more prolix, you being both in Age and Experience above me; and are well acquainted, not only with the Opinions of others, but also have seen the Customs of many, and their Cities. *B.* I shall then do it, it, and that very willingly, yet will I not unfold my own Opinion so much, as that of the Ancients, that thereby a greater Authority may be given to my discourse, as not being such as is made up with respect to this time, but taken out of the Opinions of those, who not being concerned in the present controversie, have no less eloquently than briefly given their judgment, without Hatred, Favour, or Envy, whose Case was far from these things; and their Opinions I shall especially make use of, who have not friviloufly trifled away their time, but by vertue and counsel have flourished both at home and abroad in well governed Commonwealths. But before I produce these witnesses, I would ask you some few things, that seeing we are at accord in some things of no small importance, there may be no necessity to digress from the purpose in hand, nor to stay in explaining or confirming things that are perspicuous and well known. *M.* I think we should do so, and if you please ask me. *B.* Do you not think that the time hath been, when men did dwell in Cottages, yea and in Caves, and as strangers did wander to and fro without Laws, or certain dwelling places, and did Assemble together as their fond humours did lead them, or as some Commodity, and common utility did allure them? *M.* forsooth I believe that; seeing it is consonant to the course and order of Nature, and is testified by all the Histories of all Nations almost, for *Homer* doth discribe the representation of such a Wild and Barbarous kind of life in *Sicily*, even in the time of the *Trojans.* Their Courts (saith he) do neither abound with Councils nor Judges, they dwell only in darksome Caves, and every one of them in high mountains ruleth his own House, Wife and Children, nor is any of them at leisure to Communicate his Domestick affairs to any other. About the same time also *Italy* is said to be no better civilized, as we may easily conjecture from the most fertile regions almost of the whole World, how great a solitude and wastness there were in places on this side of *Italy.* *B.* But whether do you think the vagrant and solitary life, or the Associations of men civily incorporate, most agreeable to nature? *M.* The last without all peradventure, which *utility* the Mother almost of justice and equity did first convocate; and commanded to give signs or warnings by sound of Trumpet, and to defend themselves within Walls and to shut the Gates with one Key. *B.* But, do you think that utility was the first and main cause of the association of Men? *M.* Why not, seeing I have heard from the learned, that men are Born for men. *B.* Utility indeed to some seems to be very efficacious, both in begetting and conserving the publick Society of Mankind; but if I mistake not, there is a far more venerable, or ancient cause of mens associating, and a more Antecedaneous

The due Priviledge of the Scotch Government. 7

cedaneous and Sacred bond of their Civil Community, otherwise, if every one would have a regard to his own private advantage, then surely that very utility would rather dissolve than unite humane society together. *M.* Perhaps that may be true, therefore I desire to know what other cause you will assign. *B.* A certain instinct of nature, not only in Man, but also in the more tamed sort of Beasts, that although these allurements of utility be not in them, yet do they of their own accord flock together with other Beasts of their own kind. But of these others we have no ground of debate? Surely we see this instinct by nature so deeply rooted in Man, that if any one had the affluence of all things, which contribute either for maintaining health, or pleasure and delight of the mind, yet he will think his life unpleasant without humane converse. Yea, they who out of a desire of knowledge, and an endeavour of investigating the truth, have withdrawn themselves from the multitude, and retired to secret corners, could not long endure a perpetual vexation of mind, nor, if at any time they should remit the same, could they live in solitude, but very willingly did bring forth to light their very secret studies, and as they had laboured for the publick good, they did communicate to all the fruit of their labour. But if there be any man who doth wholly take delight in solitude, and flee from converse with men, and shun it, I judge it doth rather proceed from a distemper of the mind, than from any instinct of nature, such as we have heard of *Timon* the *Athenian,* and *Bellerophon* the *Corinthian,* who (as the Poet saith) was a wandring wretch on the *Elean* Coasts, eating his own Heart, and fleeing the very Foot-steps of Men. *M.* I do not in this much dissent from you, but there is one word Nature here set down by you, which I do often use rather out of Custome, than that I understand it, and is by others so variously taken, and accommodated to so many things, that for the most part I am at a stand to what I may mainly apply it. *B.* Forsooth at present I would have no other thing to be understood thereby, than that light infused by God into our minds, for when God formed that Creature more sacred, and capable of a Celestial mind, and which might have dominion over the other Creatures, he gave not only Eyes to his Body, whereby he might evite things contrary to his condition, and follow after such as might be useful, but also he produced in his mind a certain light, whereby he might discern things filthy from honest; this light some call Nature, others the Law of Nature, for my own part, truly I think it is of a heavenly stamp, and I am fully perswaded, that Nature doth never say one thing, and Wisdom another. Moreover, God hath given us an abridgment of that Law, which might contain the whole in few words, *viz.* That we should
C love

love him with all our Soul, and our neighbours as our selves, all the Books of Holy Scripture which Treat of ordering our Conversation, do contain nothing else but an explication of this Law. *M.* You think then that no Orator or Lawyer, who might congregate dispersed men, hath been the Author of humane Society, but God only? *B.* It is so indeed, and with *Cicero,* I think there is nothing done on Earth more acceptable to the great God, who rules the World, than the associations of men legally united, which are called Civil Incorporations, whose several parts must be as compactly joyned together, as the several Members of our Body, and every one must have their proper function, to the end there may be a mutual Cooperating for the good of the whole, and a mutual propelling of injuries, and a foreseeing of advantages, and these to be Communicated for engaging the benevolence of all amongst themselves. *M.* You do not then make utility, but that Divine Law rooted in us from the beginning, to be the cause (indeed the far more worthy and Divine of the two) of mens incorporating in political Societies. *B.* I mean not indeed that to be the Mother of Equity and Justice, as some would have it, but rather the Handmaid, and to be one of the guards in Cities well constituted. *M.* Herein I also agree with you. *B.* Now as in our Bodies consisting of contrary Elements, there are Diseases, that is, perturbations, and some intestine tumults, even so there must be of necessity in these greater Bodies, that is in Cities, which also consist of various, (yea and for the most part) contrary humours, or sorts of men, and these of different ranks, conditions and natures, and which is more, of such as cannot remain one hour together approving the same things: And surely such must needs soon dissolve and come to nought; if one be not adhibited, who as a Physician may quiet such disturbances, and by a moderate and wholsom Temperament confirm the infirm parts and compesce redundant humours, and so take care of all the Members, that the weaker may not languish for want of Nutrition, nor the stronger become luxuriant too much. *M.* Truly, it must needs be so. *B.* How then shall we call him who performeth these things in a Civil Body? *B.* I am not very anxious about his name, for by what name soever he be called, I think he must be a very excellent and Divine Person, wherein the Wisdom of our Ancestors seemeth to have much foreseen, who have adorned the thing in it self most illustrious with an illustrious name. I suppose you mean *King,* of which word there is such an *Emphasis,* that it holds forth before us clearly a function in it self very great and excellent. *B.* You are very right, for we design God by that name. For we have no other more glorious name whereby we may declare the excellency

of

The due Priviledge of the Scotch *Government.*

of his glorious Nature, nor more suitable, whereby to signifie his paternal care and providence towards us. What other names shall I collect, which we Translate to denote the Function of a King? Such as Father *Æneas*, *Agamemnon*, Pastor of the People, also a Leader, Prince, Governour. By all which names such a signification is implyed, as may shew that Kings are not ordained for themselves, but for the People. Now as for the name we agree well enough: If you please, let us confer concerning the Function, insisting in the same Foot-steps we began upon. *M.* Which, I pray? *B.* Do you remember what hath been lately spoken, that an incorporation seemeth to be very like our Body, Civil Commotions like to Diseases, and a King to a Physician? if therefore we shall understand what the duty of a Physician is, I am of the Opinion, we shall not much mistake the duty of a King. *M.* It may be so, for the rest you have reckoned are very like, and seem to me very near in kin. *B.* Do not expect that I will here describe every petty thing, for the time will not permit it, neither doth the matter in hand call for it: But if briefly these agree together, you shall easily comprehend the rest. *M.* Go on then, as you are doing. *B.* The scope seemeth to be the same to us both. *M.* Which? *B.* The Health of the Body, for curing of which they are adhibited. *M.* I understand you, for the one ought to keep safe the humane Body in its state, and the other the Civil Body in its state, as far as the nature of each can bear, and to reduce into perfect Health the Body Diseased. *B.* You understand very well, for there is a twofold duty incumbent to both, the one is to preserve Health, the other is to restore it, if it become weak by sickness. *M.* I assent to you. *B.* For the Diseases of both are alike. *M.* It seemeth so. *B.* For the redundance of things hurtful, and want or scarsity of things necessary are alike noxious to both, and both the one and other Body is Cured almost in the same manner, namely either by nourishing that which is extenuate and tenderly cherishing it, or by asswaging that which is full and redundant by casting out superfluities, and exercising the Body with moderate labours. *M.* It is so, but here seems to be the difference, that the humours in the one, and manners in the other are to be reduced into a right temperament. *B.* You understand it well, for the Body politick as well as the natural hath its own proper temperament, which I think very rightly we may call Justice. For it is that which doth regard every Member, and cureth it so as to be kept in its Function. This sometimes is done by letting of Blood, sometimes by expelling of hurtful things, as by egestion; and sometimes exciting cast down and timorous minds, and comforting the weak, and so reduceth the whole

Body into that temperament I spoke of: and being reduced, exerciseth it with convenient exercises, and by a certain prescribed temperature of Labour and rest, doth preserve the restored Health as much as can be. *M.* All the rest I easily assent too, except that you place the temperament of the Body Politick in Justice: seeing temperance even by its very name and profession doth justly seem to claim these parts. *B.* I think it is no great matter on which of them you confer this honour. For seeing all Vertues, whereof the strength is best perceived in Action, are placed in a certain mediocrity and equability, so are they in some measure Connected amongst themselves, and cohere, so as it seems to be but one office in all, that is, the moderation of Lusts. Now in whatsoever kind this moderation is, it is no great matter how it be denominate: Albeit that moderation, which is placed in publick matters, and Mens mutual commerces doth seem most fitly to be understood by the name of Justice. *M.* Herein I very willingly assent to you. *B.* In the Creation of a King, I think the Ancients have followed this way, that if any among the Citizens where of any singular excellency, and seemed to exceed all others in Equity and Prudence, as is reported to be done in *Bee-Hives*, they willingly conferred the Government or Kingdom on him. *M.* It is credible to have been so. *B.* But what if none such as we have spoken of, should be found in the City? *M.* By that Law of Nature, whereof we formerly made mention, equals neither can, nor ought to Usurp Dominion: For by Nature I think it Just, that amongst these that are equal in all other things, their course of ruling and obeying should be alike. *B.* What if a People, wearied with yearly Ambition be willing to Elect some certain Person not altogether endowed with all Royal Vertues, but either famous by his Noble Descent, or Warlike Valour? will you not think that he is a lawful King? *M.* Most lawful, for the People have Power to Confer the Government on whom they please. *B.* What if we shall admit some acute Man, yet not endowed with notable skil, for Curing Diseases? shall we presently account him a Physician, as soon as he is chosen by all? *M.* Not at all; for by Learning, and the Experients of many Arts, and not by suffrages is a Man made a Physician. *B.* What maketh Artists in other Arts? *M.* I think there is one reason of all. *B.* Do you think there is any Art of Reigning or not? *M.* Why not. *B.* Can you give me a reason why you think so? *M.* I think I can, namely that same which is usually given in other Arts. *B.* What is that? *M.* Because the beginnings of all Arts proceed from experience. For whilst many did rashly and without any reason undertake to Treat of many things, and others again through exercitation and consuetude did the same more

sagaciously,

sagaciously, noticing the events on both hands, and perpending the causes thereof, some acute Men have digested a certain order of precepts, and called that Description an Art. *B.* Then by the like animadversion may not some Art of Reigning be described, as well as the Art of Physick? *M.* I think there may. *B.* Of what precepts shall it consist? *M.* I do not know at present. *B.* What if we shall find it out by comparing it with other Arts? *M.* What way? *B.* This way: There be some precepts of Grammar, of Physick and Husbandry. *M.* I understand. *B.* Shall we not call these precepts of Grammarians and Physicians Arts and Laws also, and so of others? *M.* It seems indeed so. *B.* Do not the Civil Laws seem to be certain precepts of Royal Art? *M.* They seem so. *B.* He must therefore be acquainted therewith, who would be accounted a King. *M.* It seems so. *B.* What if he have no skill therein? Albeit the People shall command him to Reign, think you that he should be called a King? *M.* You cause me here to hesitate: For if I would consent with the former discourse, the suffrages of the People can no more make him a King, than any other Artist. *B.* What think you, shall then be done? For unless we have a King chosen by suffrages, I am afraid we shall have no lawful King at all. *M.* And I fear also the same. *B.* Will you then be content that we more acurately examine what we have last set down in comparing Arts one with another? *M.* Be it so, if it so please you. *B.* Have we not called the precepts of Artists in their several Arts, Laws? *M.* We have done so. *B.* But I fear we have not done it circumspectly enough. *M.* Why? *B.* Because he would seem absurd who had skill in any Art, and yet not to be an Artist. *M.* It were so: *B.* But he that doth perform what belongs to an Art, we will account him an Artist, whether he do it naturally, or by some perpetual and constant Tenour and faculty. *M.* I think so. *B.* We shall then call him an Artist, who knows well this rational and prudent way of doing any thing well, providing he hath acquired that faculty by constant Practice. *M.* Much better than him who hath the bare precept without use and exercitation. *B.* Shall we not then account these precepts to be Art? *M.* Not at all, but a certain similitude thereof, or rather a shadow of Art? *B.* What is then that Governing faculty of Cities, which we shall call Civil Art or Science? *M.* It seems you would call it Prudence : Out of which, as from a Fountain or Spring, all Laws, providing they be useful for the preservation of humane Society, must proceed and be derived. *B.* You have hit the Nail on the Head; if this then were compleat and perfect in any person, we might say he were a King by Nature, and not by suffrages, and might resign over to him a Free Power over all things: But if we find

find not such a man, we shall also call him a King, who doth come nearest to that Eminent excellency of Nature, embracing in him a certain similitude of a true King. *M.* Let us call him so, if you please. *B.* And because we fear he be not firm enough against inordinate affections, which may, and for the most part use to decline Men from Truth, we shall adjoyn to him the Law, as it were a Colleague, or rather a Bridler of his Lusts. *M.* You do not think that a King should have an Arbitrary Power over all things. *B.* Not at all: For I remember, that he is not only a King, but also a Man, Erring in many things by Ignorance, often failing willingly, doing many things by constraint: Yea a Creature easily changeable at the blast of every Favour or Frown, which natural Vice a Magistrate useth also to increase; so that here I chiefly find that of the Comedy made true. *All by Licenſe become worſe.* Wherefore the most Prudent have thought it expedient to adjoyn to him a Law, which may either shew him the way, if he be ignorant, or bring him back again into the way, if he wander out of it: By these, I suppose, you understand, as in a representation, what I judge to be the duty of a true King. *M.* Of the cause of Creating Kings, of their name and duty you have fully satisfied me. Yet I shall not repine, if you please to add ought thereto: Albeit my mind doth hasten to hear what yet seems to remain, yet there is one thing which in all your discourse did not a little offend me, which I think should not be past over in silence, *viz.* That you seem somewhat injurious to Kings, and this very thing I did suspect in you frequently before, whilst I often heard you so profusely commend the Ancient Common-Wealths, and the City of *Venice.* *B* You did not rightly herein judge of me. For I do not so much look to the different form of Civil Government (such as was amongst the *Romans, Maſſilians, Venetians* and others, amongst whom the Authority of Laws were more Powerful, than that of Men) as to the equity of the form of Government; nor do I think it matters much, whether *King, Duke, Emperor,* or *Conſul* be the name of him who is Chiefest in Authority, providing this be granted, that he is placed in the Magistracy for the maintainance of Equity, for if the Government be lawful we must not contend for the name thereof. For he whom we call the Duke of *Venice,* is nothing else but a lawful King: and the first Consuls did not only retain the Honours of Kings, but also their Empire and Authority, this only was the difference, that not one, but two of them did Reign (which also you know was usual in all the *Lacedemonian* Kings,) who were Created or Chosen not constantly to continue in the Government, but for one Year. We must therefore always stand to what we spoke at first,

that

The due Priviledge of the Scotch Government.   13

that Kings at first were instituted for maintaining equity. If they could have holden that soveraignty in the case they had received it, they might have holden and kept it perpetually; but this is free and loosed by Laws. But (as it is with human things) the State of affairs tending to worse, the soveraign Authority which was ordained for publick utility degenerated into a proud domination. For when the lust of Kings stood instead of Laws, and men being vested with an infinite and immoderate power, did not contain themselves within bounds, but connived at many things out of favour, hatred, or self interest, the insolency of Kings made Laws to be desired. For this cause therefore Laws were made by the People, and Kings constrained to make use, not of their own licencious Wills in judgment, but of that right or priviledge which the People had conferred upon them. For they were taught by many experiences, that it was better, that their liberty should be concredited to Laws than to Kings, whereas the one might decline many ways from the Truth, but the other being deaf both to intreaties and threats, might still keep one and the same tenor. This one way of Government is to Kings prescribed, otherwise free, that they should conform their actions and speech to the Prescripts of Laws, and by the sanctions thereof divide rewards and punishments, the greatest Bonds of holding fast together human Society. And lastly, even as saith that famous Legislator, *A King should be a speaking Law, and the Law a dumb King*. M. At first you so highly praised Kings, that you made their Majesty almost glorious and sacred, but now, as if you had repented in so doing, I do not know within what strait Bonds you shut them up, and being thrust into the Prison (I may say) of Laws, you do scarce give them leave to speak. And as for my part, you have disappointed me of my expectation very far. For I expected, that (according to the most famous Historians) you should have restored the thing which is the most glorious both with God and Man, into its own splendor, either of your own accord, or at my desire in the series in your discourse, which being spoiled of all Ornaments, you have brought it into subjection, and that Authority, which through all the World is the chiefest, you having hedged in round about and made it almost so contemptible, as not to be desired by any Man in his right wits. For what Man in his right wits would not rather live as a private Man with a mean fortune, than being still in action about other Mens Affairs, to be in perpetual trouble, and neglecting his own Affairs, to order the whole Course of his Life according to other Mens Rules? But if that be the Terms of Government every where proposed, I fear there will be a greater scarcity of Kings found, than was of Bishops in the first Infancy of our Religion. Nor do I much wonder, if

Kings

Kings be regarded according to this plate form, being but Men taken from Feeding Cattle, and from the Plough, who took upon them that glorious Dignity. *B.* Consider I pray you, in how great an Error you are, who does think that Kings were Created by People and Nations not for Justice, but for pleasure, and does think there can be no Honour, where Wealth and Pleasures abound not; wherein consider how much you diminish their Grandeur. Now that you may the more easily understand it; compare any one King of those you have seen apparrelled like a Childs puppet brought forth with a great deal of Pride and a great many attendants, meerly for vain ostentation, the representation whereof you miss in that King whom we describe. Compare, I say, some one of those, who were famous of old, whose memory doth even yet live, flourisheth and is renowned to all Posterity. Indeed they were such as I have now been describing. Have you never heard what an old woman petitioning *Philip* King of *Macedon* to hear her Cause, answered him, he having said to her, he had no leasure, to which she replied, then cease, (said she) to be King? have you never heard, (I say) that a King victorious in so many Battles, and Conqueror of so many Nations, admonished to do his duty by a Poor old wife, obeyed, and acknowledged that it was the duty of Kings so to do? Compare then this *Philip* not only with the greatest Kings that are now in *Europe*, but also with all that can be remembred of old, you shall surely find none of them comparable to those either for Prudence, Fortitude, or activity; few equal to them for largeness of Dominions. If I should enumerate *Agesilaus, Leonidas,* and the rest of the *Lacedemonian* Kings (O how great Men were they) I shall seem to utter but obsolete Examples. Yet one saying of a *Lacedemonian* Maid I cannot pass over with silence, her Name was *Gorgo* the Daughter of *Cleomedes,* she seeing a Servant pulling off the Stockings of an *Asian Ghuest,* and running to her Father cry'd out, Father, the Ghuest hath no Hands; from which Speech of that Maid you may easily judge of the *Lacedemonian* discipline and domestick Custom of their Kings. Now those who proceeded out of this rustick, but couragious way of life, did very great things: but those who were bred in the *Asiatick* way, lost by their luxury and sloth the great dominions given their Ancestors. And, that I may lay aside the Ancients. Such a one was *Pelagius* not long ago among the People of *Galicia,* who was the first that weakned the *Saracen* forces in *Spain,* yet him and all his the Grave did inclose, yet of him the *Spanish* Kings are not ashamed, accounting it their greatest glory to be descended of him. But seeing this place doth call for a more large discourse, let us return from whence we have digressed greffed. For I defire to fhew you with the firft that I promifed, namely that this form of Government hath not been contrived by me, but feems to have been the fame to the moft famous men in all Ages, and I fhall fhew briefly you the fpring from whence I have drawn thefe things. The Books of *M. Tullius Cicero* which are intitled of *Offices* are by common confent of all accounted moft praife worthy, in the fecond Book thereof thefe words are fet down *verbatim*, it feems as *Herodotus* faith that of old, well bred Kings were created, not amongft the *Medes* only, but alfo amongft our Anceftors for executing of Juftice, for whilft at firft the People were oppreffed by thofe that had greateft wealth, they betook themfelves to fome one who was eminent for vertue, who whilft he kept off the weakeft from injuries, eftablifhing equity, he hemmed in the higheft with the loweft by equal Laws to both. And the reafon of making Laws was the fame as of the Creation of Kings, for it is requifite that juftice be always equal, for otherwife it were not juftice. If this they did obtain from one good and juft Man, they were therewith well pleafed, when they did not occur, Laws were made, which by one and the fame voice might fpeak to all alike. This then indeed is evident, that thofe were ufually chofen to govern, of whofe juftice the People had a great opinion. Now this was added, that thefe Rulers or Kings might be accounted prudent, there was nothing that Men thought they could not obtain from fuch Rulers. I think, you fee from thefe words, what *Cicero* judgeth to be the reafon of requiring both Kings and Laws. I might here commend *Zenophon* a witnefs requiring the fame, no lefs famous in War-like affairs, than in the ftudy of Phylofopy, but that I know you are fo well acquainted with his Writings, as that you have all his fentences marked. I pafs at prefent *Plato* and *Ariftotle*, albeit I am not ignorant how much you have them in eftimation. For I had rather adduce for confirmation Men famous in a middle degree of affairs, than out of Schools. Far lefs do I think fit to produce a Stoick King, fuch as by *Seneca* in *Thyeftes* is defcribed: Not fo much becaufe that Idea of a King is not perfect, as becaufe that Examples of a good Prince may be rather impreffed in the Mind, than at any time hoped for. But left in thofe I have produced there might be any ground of calumny, I have not fet before you Kings out of the *Scythian* folitude, who did either ungird their own Horfes, or did other fervile work, which might be very far from our manner of living: but even out of *Greece*, and fuch, who in thefe very times, wherein the *Grecians* did moft flourifh in all liberal Sciences, did rule the greateft Nations, or well governed Cities; and did fo rule, that whilft they were alive were in very great efteem amongft their People, and being dead left to Pofterity a famous

D memory

memory of themselves. *M.* If now you ask me what my judgment is, I scarce dare confess to you either mine inconstancy or timidity, or by what other name it shall please you to call that vice. For as often as I read these things you have now recited in the most famous Historians, or hear the same commended by very wise Men, whose Authority I dare not decline: and that they are approved by all good and honest Men to be not only true, equitable and sincere, but also seem strong and splendid. Again as oft as I cast mine Eyes on the neatness and elegancy of our times, that antiquity seemeth to have been venerable and sober, but yet rude, and not sufficiently polished, but of these things we may perhaps speak of hereafter at more leasure. Now if it please you, go on to prosecute what you have begun. *B.* May it please you then that we recollect briefly what hath been said? So shall we understand best what is past, and if ought be rashly granted, we shall very soon retract it. *M.* Yes indeed. *B.* First of all then we agree, that Men by nature are made to live in society together, and for a communion of life. *M.* That is agreed upon. *B.* That a King also chosen to maintain that society is a Man eminent in Vertue. *M.* It is so. *B.* And as the discords of Men amongst themselves brought in the necessity of creating a King, so the Injuries of *Kings* done against their Subjects were the cause of desiring Laws. *M.* I acknowledg that. *B.* We held Laws to be a Proof of the Art of Government, even as the Precepts of Physitians are of the Medicinal Art. *M.* It is so. *B.* But it seems to be more safe (because in neither of the two have we set down any singular and exact Skill of their several Arts) that both do, as speedily as may be, heal by these Prescripts of Art. *M.* It is indeed safest. *B.* Now the Precepts of the Medicinal Art are not of one kind. *M.* How? *B.* For some of them are for preservation of health, others for restoration thereof. *M.* Very right. *B.* What say you of the governing Art? *M.* I think there be as many kinds. *B.* Next then it seems, that we consider it. Do you think, that Physitians can so exactly have Skill of all diseases and of their remedies, as nothing more can be required for their cure? *M.* Not at all, for many new kinds of Diseases arise almost in every Age, and new remedies for each of them, almost every year are by Men's Industry found out, or brought from far Countries. *B.* What think you of the Laws of Commonwealths. *M.* Surely their case seems to be the same. *B.* Therefore neither Physitians, nor *Kings* can evite or cure all Diseases of Common-wealths, by the Precepts of their Arts, which are delivered to them in Writ. *M.* I think indeed they cannot. *B.* What if we shall farther try of what things Laws may be established in Common-wealths, and what cannot be comprehended within Laws. *M.* That will be worth

The due Priviledge of the Scotch Government. 17

worth our pains. *B.* There seems to be very many and weighty things, which cannot be contained within Laws. First, all such things, as fall into the deliberation of the time to come. *M.* All indeed. *B.* next, many things already past, such are these wherein truth is sought by conjectures, confirmed by Witnesses, or extorted by Torments. *M.* Yes indeed. *B.* In unfolding then these Questions, what shall the King do? *M.* I see here there is no need of a long discourse, seeing Kings do not so arrogate the Supream Power in those things which are instituted with respect to the time to come, that of their own accord they call to Council some of the most prudent. *B.* What say you of those things which by conjectures are found out, and made out by Witnesses, such as are the Crimes of Murther, Adultery and Witchcraft? *M.* These are examined by the skill of Lawyers, discovered by diligence, and these I find to be for the most part left to the judgment of Judges. *B.* And perhaps very right; for if a King would needs be at the private causes of each Subject, when shall he have time to think upon Peace and War, and those affairs which maintain and preserve the safety of the Common-wealth? And lastly when shall he get leave to rest? *M.* neither would I have the cognition of every thing to be brought unto a King, neither can one man be sufficient for all the causes of all men, if they be brought unto him: that Council no less wise than necessary doth please me exceeding well, which the Father in Law of *Moses* gave him in dividing amongst many the Burden of hearing Causes, whereof I shall not speak much, seeing the History is known to all. *B.* But I think, these Judges must Judg according to Law. *M.* They must indeed do so. But as I conceive, there be but few things, which by Laws may be provided against, in respect of those which cannot be provided against.

B. There is another thing of no less difficulty, because all these things which call for Laws, cannot be comprehended by certain prescriptions. *M.* How so? *B.* Lawyers, who attribute very much to their own Art, and who would be accounted the Priests of Justice, do confess that there is so great a multitude of affairs, that it may seem almost infinite, and say that daily arise new crimes in Cities, as it were several kinds of Ulcers, what shall a Law-giver do herein, who doth accommodate Laws both to things present and preterite? *M.* Not much, unless he be some Divine-like Person. *B.* Another difficulty doth also Occur, and that not a small one, that in so great an Inconstancy of humane Frailty, no Art can almost prescribe any thing altogether stable and firm. *M.* There is nothing more true than that. *B.* It seemeth then most safe to trust a skilful Physician in the Health of the Patient, and also the King in the State of the Common-wealth. For a Phyfitian without the rule of Art will oftentimes Cure a weak Patient, either by confenting thereto, or againſt his will: And a King doth either perſwade a new Law uſeful to his Subjects, or elſe may impoſe it againſt their will. *M.* I do not ſee what may hinder him therein. *B.* Now ſeeing both the one and the other do theſe things, do you think that beſides the Law, either of them makes his own Law? *M.* It ſeems that both doth it by Art. For we have before concluded not that to be Art which confiſts of precepts, but Vertue contained in the mind, which the Artiſt uſually makes uſe of in handling the matter which is ſubject to Arts. Now I am glad (ſeeing you ſpeak ingenuouſly) that you being conſtrained, as it were, by an interdiction of the very truth, do ſo far reſtore the King from whence he was by force dejected. *B.* Stay, you have not yet heard all. There is another inconvenience in the Authority of Laws. For the Law being as it were a pertinacious, and a certain rude Exactor of duty, thinks nothing right, but what it ſelf doth command. But with a King, there is an excuſe of Infirmity and Temerity, and place of Pardon left for one found in an Error. The Law is Deaf, Cruel and Inexorable. A Young man Pleads the frailty of his Years, a Woman the infirmity of Her Sex, another his Poverty, Drunkenneſs, Affection. What ſaith the Law to theſe excuſes? Go Officer or Serjeant, convene a Band of Men, Hoodwink him, Scourge him, Hang him on a Tree. Now you know how dangerous a thing it is, in ſo great a Humane frailty, to have the hope of Safety placed in Innocency alone. *M.* In very Truth you tell me a thing full of Hazard. *B.* Surely as oft as theſe things come into mind, I perceive ſome not a little troubled. *M.* You ſpeak true. *B.* When therefore I ponder with my ſelf what is before paſt as granted, I am afraid left the compariſon of a Phyſitian and of a King in this caſe ſeem not pertinently enough introduced. *M.* In what caſe? *B.* When we have liberated both of the ſervitude of precepts, and given them almoſt a free liberty of Curing. *M.* What doth herein eſpecially offend you? *B.* When you hear it, you will then judge. Two cauſes are by us ſet down, why it is not expedient for a People that Kings be looſed from the bonds of Laws, namely, love and hatred, which drive the minds of Men to and fro in judging. But in a Phyſitian it is not to be feared, left he fail through love, ſeeing he expecteth a reward from his Patient being reſtored to Health. But if a Patient underſtand that his Phyſitian is ſolicited by Intreaties, Promiſes and Mony againſt his Life, he may call another Phyſitian, or if he can find none other, I think it is more ſafe to ſeek ſome remedy from Books how Deaf ſoever, than from a corrupt Phyſitian. Now becauſe

we

we have complained of the Cruelty of Laws, look if we underſtand one another ſufficiently. *M.* How ſo? *B.* We judged an excellent King, ſuch as we may more ſee in mind, than with Bodily Eyes, not to be bound by any Laws. *M.* By none. *B.* Wherefore? *M.* I think, becauſe, according to *Paul*, he ſhould be a Law to himſelf and to others, that he may expreſs in life what is by Law enjoyned. *B.* You judge rightly; and that you may perhaps the more admire, ſeveral Ages before *Paul*, *Ariſtotle* did ſee the ſame, following Nature as a Leader, which therefore I ſay, that you may ſee the more clearly what hath been proved before, to wit, that the Voice of God and Nature is the ſame. But that we may proſecute our purpoſe. What ſhall we ſay they had a reſpect unto, who firſt made Laws? *M.* Equity I think, as hath been ſaid before. *B.* I do not now demand that, what end they had before them, but rather what pattern they propoſed to themſelves? *M.* Albeit perhaps I underſtand that, yet I would have you to explain it, that you may confirm my judgment, if I rightly take it up, if not, you may amend my Error. *B.* You know, I think, what the dominion is of the mind over the Body. *M.* I ſeem to know it. *B.* You know this alſo, what ever we do not raſhly, that there is a certain *Idea* thereof firſt in our minds, and that it is a great deal more perfect than the works to be done, which according to that Pattern the chiefeſt Artiſts, do frame, and as it were expreſs. *M.* That indeed I find by experience both in ſpeaking and writing, and perceive no leſs words in my mind, than my mind in things wanting. For neither can our mind, ſhut up in this dark and troubled Priſon of the Body, perceive the ſubtilty of all things; nor can we ſo endure in our mind the repreſentation of things however foreſeen in diſcourſe with others, ſo as they are not much inferiour to theſe which our intellect hath formed to it ſelf. *B.* What ſhall we ſay then which they ſet before them, who made Laws? *M.* I ſeem almoſt to underſtand what you would be at. Namely, that they in Council had an *Idea* of that perfect King, and that they did expreſs a certain Image, not of the Body but of the mind, according to that foreſaid *Idea*, as near as they could. And would have that to be inſtead of Laws which he is to think might be good and equitable. *M.* You rightly underſtand it. For that is the very thing I would ſay. But now I would have you to conſider what manner of King that is which we have conſtitute at firſt, was he not one firm and ſtedfaſt againſt Hatred, Love, Wrath, Envy, and other perturbations of the mind? *M.* We did indeed imagine him to be ſuch a one: Or believed him to have been ſuch to thoſe Ancients. *B.* But do Laws ſeem to have been made according to the *Idea* of him? *M.* Nothing

thing more likely. *B.* A good King then is no less severe and inexorable, than a good Law. *M.* He is even as severe: But since I can change neither, or ought to desire it, yet I would slacken both somewhat, if I can. *B.* But God desires not that mercy be shewed even to the Poor in judgment, but commandeth us to respect that one thing which is Just and Equal, and to pronounce Sentence accordingly. *M.* I do acknowledge that, and by truth am overcome. Seeing therefore it is not lawful to loose Kings from the Bonds of Laws, who shall then be the Law-giver? Whom shall we give him as a Pedagogue? *B.* whom do you think fittest to perform this duty? *M.* If you ask at me. I think the King himself. For in all other Arts almost we see their precepts are given by the Artists; whereof they make use, as it were of comments, for confirming their Memory, and putting others in mind of their duty. *B.* On the contrary I see no difference: Let us grant that a King is at liberty and solved from the Laws, shall we grant him the Power to command Laws? For no Man will willingly lay Bonds and Fetters upon himself. And I know not whether it be better to leave a Man without Bonds, or to Fetter him with slight Bonds, because he may rid himself thereof when he pleases. *M.* But when you concredit the Helm of Government rather to Laws than to Kings, beware I pray you, left you make him a Tyrant, whom by name you make a King, who with Authority doth oppress and with Fetters and Imprisonment doth bind, and so let him be sent back to the Plough again, or to his former condition, yet free of Fetters. *B.* Brave words: I impose no Lord over him, but I would have it in the Peoples Power, who gave him the Authority over themselves, to prescribe to him a Model of his Government, and that the King may make use of that Justice, which the People gave him over themselves. This I crave. I would not have these Laws to be by force imposed, as you interpret it, but I think that by a Common Council with the King, that should be generally established, which may generally tend to the good of all. *M.* You will then grant this Liberty to the People? *B.* Even to the People indeed, unless perhaps you be of another mind. *M.* Nothing seems less equitable. *B.* Why so? *M.* You know that saying, a Beast with many Heads. You know, I suppose, how great the temerity and inconstancy of a People is. *B.* I did never imagine that that matter ought to be granted to the judgment of the whole People in general, but that near to our Custom, a select number out of all Estates may convene with the King in Council. And then how soon an overture by them is made, that it be deferred to the Peoples judgment. *M.* I understand well enough your advice. But by this so careful a Cau-

tion

tion you seem to help your self nothing. You will not have a King loosed from Laws, why? Because, I think, within Man two most Cruel Monsters lust and wrath are in a continual conflict with reason. Laws have been greatly desired, which might repress their boldness, and reduce them too much insulting, to regard a just Government. What wil. these Counsellors given by the People do? Are they not troubled by that same intestine conflict? Do they not conflict with the same evils as well as the King? The more then you adjoyn to the King as Assessors, there will be the greater number of Fools, from which you see what is to be expected. *B.* But I expect a far other thing than you suppose. Now I shall tell you why I do expect it. First, it is not altogether true what you suppose, *viz.* That the Assembling together of a multitude is of no purpose, of which number there will perhaps be none of a profound wit: for not only do many see more and understand more than one of them apart, but also more than one, albeit he exceed their wit and prudence. For a multitude for the most part doth better judge of all things, than single persons apart. For every one apart have some particular Vertues, which being United together make up one excellent Vertue, which may be evidently seen in Physicians Pharmacies, and especially in that Antidote, which they call Mithredate. For therein are many things of themselves hurtful apart, which being compounded and mingled together make a wholesom Remedy against Poyson. In like manner in some Men slowness and lingring doth hurt, in others a Pricipitant Temerity, both which being mingled together in a multitude make a certain Temperament and Mediocrity, which we require to be in every kind of Vertue. *M.* Be it so, seeing you will have it so, let the People make Laws and Execute them; and let Kings be as it were Keepers of Registers. But when Laws seem to Clash, or are not exact and perspicuous enough in Sanctions, will you allow the King no interest or medling here, especially since you will have him to judge all things by written Laws, there must needs ensue many absurdities. And, that I may make use of a very common example of that Law commended in the Schools. If a Stranger scale a Wall, let him die. What can be more absurd than this, that the Author of a publick safety (who have thrust down the enemies pressing hard to be up) should be drawn to punishment, as if he had in Hostility attempted to scall the walls. *B.* That is nothing. *M.* You approve then that old saying, the highest justice is the highest injury. *B.* I do indeed. If any thing of this kind come into debate, there is need of a meek interpreter, who may not suffer the Laws which are made for the good of all to be calamitous to good Men, and deprehend in no Crime. *B.* You

are

are very right, neither is there any thing else by me sought in all this dispute, (if you have sufficiently noticed it) than that Ciceronian Law might be venerable and inviolable. *Salus Populi suprema Lex esto.* If then any such thing shall come into debate, so that it be clear what is good and just, the Kings duty will be to advert that the Law may reach that Rule I spoke of, but you in behalf of Kings seem to require more, than the most imperious of them assume. For you know that these kind of Questions is usually referred to Judges, when Law seemeth to require one thing, and the Law-giver another; even as these Laws which arise from an ambiguous right, or from the Discord of Laws amongst themselves. Therefore in such cases most grievous contentions of Advocates arise in Judicatories, and Orators precepts are diligently produced. *M.* I know that to be done which you say. But in this Case no less Wrong seems to be done to Laws than to Kings. For I think it better to end that Debate presently, from the Saying of one good Man, than to grant the Power of darkning, rather than interpreting Laws to subtle Men, and sometimes to crafty Knaves; for whilst not only Contention ariseth betwixt Advocate for the Causes of Parties contending, but also for Glory, Contests are nourished in the mean time, Right or Wrong, Equity or Inequity is called in question; and what we deny to a King, we grant to Men of inferior Rank, who study more to debate, than to find out the Truth. *B.* You seem to me forgetful of what we lately agreed upon. *M.* What is that? *B.* That all things are to be so freely granted to an excellent King, as we have described him, that there might be no need of any Laws. But whilst this honour is conferred to one of the People, who is not much more excellent than others, or even inferior to some, that free and loose Licence from Laws is dangerous. *M.* But what ill doth that to the interpretation of Law. *B.* Very much. Perhaps you do not consider, that in other words we restore to him that infinite and immoderate Power, which formerly we denied to a King, namely, that according to his own Hearts lust he may turn all things upside-down. *M.* If I do that, then certainly I do it imprudently. *B.* I shall tell you more plainly, that you may understand it. When you grant the interpretation of Laws to a King, you grant him such a Licence, as the Law doth not tell what the Law-giver meaneth, or what is good and equal for all in general, but what may make for the Interpreters benefit, so that he may bend it to all actions for his own benefit or advantage, as the *Lesbian* Rule. *Ap. Claudius* in his *Decemviratus*, made a very just Law, that in a liberal Cause or Plea, sureties should be granted for liberty. What more clearly could have been spoken. But by interpreting the same

Author

Author made his own Law useless. You see; I suppose how much liberty you give a Prince by one cast, namely, that what he pleaseth the Law doth say, what pleaseth him not, it doth not say. If we shall once admit this, it will be to no purpose to make good Laws for teaching a good Prince his duty; and hemm in an ill King. Yea let me tell you more plainly, it would be better to have no Laws at all, than that freedom to steal should be tolerate, and also honoured under pretext of Law. *M*. Do you think that any King will be so impudent, that he will not at all have any regard of the fame and opinion that all Men have of him? Or that he will be so forgetful of his Subjects, that he will degenerate into their Pravity, whom he hath restrained by ignominy, imprisonment, confiscation of Goods, and in a word with very grievous punishments? *B*. Let us not believe that these things will be, if they had not been done long ago, and that to the exceeding great hurt of the whole World. *M*. Where do you tell these things were done? *B*. Do you ask, where? As if all the Nations in Europe did not only see, but feel also how much mischief hath the immoderate Power, and unbridled Tyranny of the *Pope* of *Rome* brought upon human Affairs. Even that Power which from small beginning and seemingly honest he had got, every Man doth know that no less can be feared by unwary Persons. At first, Laws were proposed to us, not only drawn out of the innermost secrets of Nature, but given by God himself, explained by the Prophets from the holy Spirit, at last by the Son of God, and by the same God confirmed, committed to the writings of those praise worthy men, expressed in their Life, and sealed with their Blood. Neither is there in the whole Law any other place more carefully, commendably, or more clearly delivered, than that of the Office of Bishops. Now seeing it is lawful to no man to add any thing to these Laws, to abrogate or derogate ought therefrom, or to change any thing therein, there did remain but one interpretation, and whilst the Pope did arrogate it, he not only did oppress the rest of the Churches, but claimed a Tyranny the most cruel of all that ever were, daring to command not only Men but Angels also, plainly reducing Christ into order, if this be not to reduce him into order, that what thou wilt have done in Heaven, in Earth and amongst the damned in Hell, be ratified: what Christ hath commanded, let it be ratified, if thou wilt; for if the Law seem to make but little for your behoof, interpreting it thus you may back bend it, so that not only by your Mouth, but also according to the judgment of your Mind Christ is constrained to speak. Christ therefore speaking by the Mouth of the Pope, *Pipin* is set in *Childericks* place of Government, *Ferdinandus* of *Arragon*

gon substitute to *John* King of *Navare*: the Son arose in Arms against his Father, and Subjects against their King. Christ is full of Poyson, then he is forced by Witches, so that he killeth *Henry* of *Luxemburg* by Poyson. *M.* I have heard these things often before, but I desire to hear more plainly somewhat of that interpretation of Laws. *B.* I shall offer you one Example, from which you may easily understand, how much this whole kind is able to do. The Law is, a Bishop must be the Husband of one Wife, than which Law what is more clear, and what may be said more plain? One Wife, (saith the Law) one Church, (saith the Pope) such is his interpretation. As if that Law were made not to repress the Lusts of Bishops but their Avarice. Now this Explanation, albeit it saith nothing to the purpose, yet doth contain a judgment honest and pious, if he had not vitiated that Law again by another interpretation. What doth therefore the Pope devise for excuse? It varieth (saith he) in regard of persons, cases, places and times. Some are of that eminent disposition, that no number of Churches can satisfie their Pride. Some Churches again are so poor, that they cannot maintain him who was lately a begging Monk, if he have now a Mitre, if he would maintain the name of a Bishop. There is a reason invented from that crafty interpretation of the Law, that they may be called Bishops of one Church, or other Churches given them in *Commendam*, and all may be robbed. Time would fail me, if I should reckon up the cheats, which are dayly excogitate against one Law. But albeit these things be most unbeseeming as well the name of a Pope, as of a Christian, yet their Tyranny rests not here. For such is the nature of all things, that when they once begin to fall, they never stay until they fall headlong into destruction. Will you have me to shew you this by a famous Example? Do you not remember upon any of the *Roman* Emperors blood who was more cruel and wicked than *C. Caligula*? *M.* There was none that I know of. *B.* Now what was his most nefarious villany think you? I do not speak of those deeds which Popes do reckon up in some reserved cases, but in the rest of his life. *M.* I do not at present remember. *B.* What do you think of that, that having called upon his Horse, he invited him to sup with him? Set a golden grain of Barley before him, and made him Consul? *M.* Indeed it was most impiously done. *B.* What think you of that, how he made the same Horse his Colleague in the Priesthood? *M.* Do you tell me that in good earnest? *B.* Indeed in good earnest, nor do I admire that these things seem to you feigned. But that *Roman Jupiter* of ours hath done such things, that those things done by *Caligula* may seem true to Posterity. I say Pope *Julius* the third, who seems contending with *C. Caligula*

ligula a most wicked wretch for preheminency of impiety. *M.* What did he of that Kind? *B.* He made his Ape-keeper, a Man almost more vile than the vilest Beast, his Colleague in the Papary. *M.* Perhaps there was another cause of choosing him. *B.* Some are reported indeed, but I have picked out the most honest. Seeing then so great a contempt not only of the Priesthood, but also a forgetfulness of humanity arise from this freedom of interpreting Laws, beware you think that to be a small Power. *M.* But the Antients seem not to have thought it so great a business of interpreting, as you would have it seem to be: Which by by this one argument may be understood, because the *Roman* Emperours granted it to Lawyers: which one reason doth overturn your whole tedious dispute, nor doth it only refute what you spoke of the greatness of that Power, but also that which you most shun, it perspicuously declareth, what Power they granted to others of answering rightly, was not denied to themselves, if they had been pleased to exerce that office, or could have done it by reason of greater affairs. *B.* As for those *Roman* Emperours, whom the Soldiers did choose indeliberately, and without any regard to the common good of all. These fall not under this notion of Kings which we have described, so that by those that were most wicked were they choosen who for the most part were most wicked, or else laid hold upon the Government by violence. Now I do not reprehend them for granting Power to Lawyers to interpret the Law. And albeit that Power be very great, as I have said before, it is notwithstanding more safely concredited to them to whom it cannot be an instrument of Tyranny. Moreover it was concredited to many whom mutual reverence did hold within the bounds of duty, that if one decline from equity, he might be refuted by another, And if they should have all agreed together into fraud, the help of the Judge was above them, who was not obliged to hold for Law what ever was given by Lawyers for an Answer. And over all was the Emperour, who might punish the breach of Laws. They being astricted by so many Bonds were hemmed in, and did fear a more grievous punishment, than any reward of fraud they could expect: you see, I suppose then that the danger to be feared from such kind of Men was not so great. *M.* Have you no more to say of a King? *B.* First, if you please, let us collect together, what is already spoken, so that the more easily we may understand, if any thing be omitted. *M.* I think we should do so. *B.* We seemed to be at accord sufficiently concerning the origine and cause of creating Kings, and making Laws, but of the Lawgiver not so: but at last, though somewhat unwillingly, I seem'd to have consented, being enforced by the strength of truth

Truth. *M.* Certainly you have not only taken from a King the Power of commanding Laws, but also of interpreting them, even whilst I as an Advocate strongly protested against it. Wherein I am afraid, if the Matter come to publick hearing, lest I be accused of Prevarication, for having so easily suffered a good Cause, as it seemed at first, to be wrung out of my Hands. *B.* Be of good Courage, for if any accuse you of Prevarication in this Case, I promise to be your Defence. *M.* Perhaps we will find that shortly. *B.* There seems to be many kinds of Affairs which can be comprehended within no Laws, whereof we laid over a part on ordinary Judges, and a part on the Kings Council by the Kings Consent. *M.* I do remember we did so indeed. And when you was doing that, wot you what came into my Mind? *B.* How can I, unless you tell me? *M.* Methought you made Kings in a manner like Stone Seals, which for the most part so seem to lean on the Tops of Pillars, as if they did sustain the whole Fabrick: whereas in effect they bear no more Burthen than any other Stone. *B.* What! good Advocate of Kings, do you complain that I lay on them a little Burthen, seeing both Day and Night they do nothing else than seek out others to bear Burthen with them, or upon whom they may altogether lay the Burthen, and so disburden themselves. And in the mean time you seem to take it in ill part, that I afford them Help, labouring under their Burthen. *M.* I also very willingly admit these Auxiliaries, but such would I have as may serve, but not command, such as may shew the way, but not lead in the way, or more truly draw or rush them forward as some warlike Engine, and leave a King no other Power but to assent to them. Therefore I presently expect, that having ended our Discourse concerning a King, you would step aside to speak of Tyrants, or some where-else. For you have inclosed a King within so narrow Bounds, that I am afraid, lest, if we tarry longer therein, you drive him out of his greatest Wealth and highest Dignity, and banish him as it were into some desert Island, where being spoiled of all his Honours, he wax old in Poverty and Misery. *B.* You feared, as you pretend, the Crime of Prevarication; but I am afraid, lest in calumniating you wrong the King, whom you endeavour to defend. First, I would not have him to be idle, unless you would appoint idle Master-builders: Secondly, you deprive him of good Ministers and Friends, whom I have adjoyned unto him, not as Keepers, but would have them called by him to bear a part of his Labour, and these being driven away, you surround him with a Band of Knaves, who make him to be feared by his Subjects, neither do you think he

will

will be formidable, unless we allow him a great Power of doing Wrong. I would have him to be by his Subjects beloved, not to be guarded by the Terror, but good Will of his Subjects, which Arms alone do make Kings Invincible, unless you gainsay this, I trust I shall shortly prove it. For I shall lead him out of these you call Straits into Light; and by one Law shall give him so much Authority and Enlargement, that if he desires more, he may seem impudent. *M.* Indeed I long to hear that. *B.* I shall then fall upon that Matter, that I may satisfie your Desire as soon as I can. A little before we have confessed, that no Law can be so accurately cautioned concerning any Affair, but that malicious Subtlety may invent some Fraud. This perhaps will be the better understood by the Example already proposed. By the Law, it is ordained, that no Parents transmit their Benefices to their Bastards. Here in effect the Law seems clear, yet a Cheat is found out; that the Father substitutes some other Man, and that he may deliver that same Benefice to the Bastard of the former Possessor. Thereafter, when as it was carefully ordained by Law, that the Son should by no means enjoy that Benefice which his Father had possessed before: yet by this Caution it was never a whit the better. For against that Law a Paction was found out among Priests, that each of them should substitute the Son of the other in his Office. And when that was also forbidden, the Law was also eluded by another kind of Cheat: a pretender was set up against the Father, who might pretend he had a Right to that Benefice. Whilst the Father seemingly is a contending with this supposed Sycophant, the Son doth petition the Pope for the Benefice, if so be that the Right unto that Benefice belong not to either of the Parties contending for it, and so the Son, by his Fathers Prevarication, doth enjoy his Fathers Benefice, and overcometh both the Parties, who willingly and freely yield up their Plea. Thus you see how many kinds of Cheats are invented against one Law. *M.* I see it. *B.* Do not Lawgivers seem to do altogether the same herein which Physicians do, who whilst they endeavour, by applying a Plaister to compesce the Eruptions of Flegm, or of some other hurtful Humor, the Humor restrained in one place, seeks Issue in many places at once; and as a certain Hydra having one Head cut off, many Heads start up in place of one. *M.* Nothing more like. *B.* What was incumbent for a Physitian to do at first, for freeing the whole Body at once of peccant Humors, ought not the Politick Physitian do the same in this Case, for freeing the whole Common-wealth of evil Manners? *M.* I think that to be the right way of Cure, albeit it be difficult. *B.* And if this can be obtained, ed, I think there would be need of few Laws. *M.* It is indeed so. *B.* Doth not he alone seem to confer more for the Publick Good, who can apply this Remedy, than all the Conventions of all Estates met for making of Laws? *M.* Doubtless far more. But that I may make use of the Comick Poets Words, Who is able to undertake so weighty a Charge? *B.* What if we shall lay it over on the King? *M.* Merrily spoken indeed. What was soon done and easie, you have committed to the whole People; but if any thing be difficult and intricate, you will lay it over upon the King alone, as if you thought him not sufficiently bound, tying him round about with so many Fetters, unless you lay upon him a most grievous Burthen, under which he may also succumb. *B.* It is not so, but we contend for a Business easie for him to be done; we beseech, he would suffer himself to be exorable. *M.* What is that, I pray? *B.* That as Fathers ought to carry towards their Children, so in all his Life he would behave himself towards his Subjects, whom he ought to account as Children. *M.* What is that to the purpose in hand? *B.* Surely this one is certainly the chiefest Remedy against corrupt Manners, and lest you suppose that it is an Invention of mine, here what *Claudianus* saith. Thou King, must as a Father Rule thy Subjects, and no less have a care of all than of thy self; let not thy own Desire only move thee, but also the Publick Desires of thy People. If thou commandest, ought to be done by all, and to be obeyed, obey the same first thy self. Then will the People become the more observant of Equity; nor will refuse to bear any Burthen, when they see their King himself obedient to what he commands. The whole World doth act conform to the Example of a King. The Laws of Kings prevail not so much to incline Mens Minds unto Obedience, as the Conversation of the Rulers. For the fluctuating Multitude doth always change as their Prince doth. Do not Imagine that the Poet pregnant for understanding and learning did in vain believe so great force to be herein, for People are so addicted to the imitation of Kings, in whom any Image of Honesty doth shine or appear, and so endeavour to express their manners, that whose Vertue they admire, they endeavour also to imitate some of their Vices in Speech, Apparel in deport. But in conforming themselves to the King in gesture, manners of Speech they not only desire to imitate him, but also by flattery they insinuate themselves into the minds of great ones, and by these Arts they hunt after Riches, Honour and Preferment, because they know we have it by Nature, that we Love not only our selves, and our own concerns, but embrace our own likeness though vicious in others. Now that which we demand not Wickedly and Arrogantly, gently, but by Entreaty endeavour to obtain, hath a far greater force than the Threatnings of Laws, the Ostentation of Punishments, or Armies of Souldiers. This reduceth a People without force into Modesty, conciliateth to a King his Subjects good Liking, increaseth and maintaineth the publick Tranquility, and the Wealth of every one severally. Let therefore a King carefully consider, that he is set on the Theatre of the World, and for a Spectacle proposed to all, so as no Word or Deed of his can be concealed. The Vices of Kings can never be kept secret. For the Supream Light of Fate suffers nothing to lye hid in Obscurity, and Fame enters into all secret Places, and finds out obscure Corners. O how much doth it concern Kings to be circumspect on all hands, seeing neither their Vices nor their Vertues can be concealed, nor yet without a great universal Change of Affairs. But if any do yet doubt, what great Importance there is in the Conversation of a Prince, for the Emendation of the publick Discipline, let him take but a View of the small beginning of the State of *Rome*. That rude People consisting of Shepherds and Country Inhabitants, I shall not say worse, naturally fierce, having got a very couragious King, and having pitched once their Tents, for soliciting the Peace of the Neighbouring Nations, and provoking them to fight, how much do you think of Hatred and Fear was bred in their Neighbours? When again that very same People had set over them a pious and just King, they were so suddenly changed, that being wholly devoted to the Worship of their Gods, and to Acts of Justice, that to wrong them their Neighbours judged it a Crime, even those very Neighbours, I say, whose Lands before they had laid waste, whose Cities they had burnt, and their Children and Kinsmen they had carried away into Bondage. Now if in that Barbarity of Manners, and Rudeness of Times, *Numa Pompilius* (who a little before was brought out of another Nation at Enmity with them, and made King) could do so much: what shall we expect, or rather, what shall we not expect of those Princes, who being supported by Affinity, Vassals, and much Wealth left them by their Ancestors, obtain the Government? And are born and brought up in expectation thereof. Now how much should it stir up their Minds unto Vertue, that they hope to have the Praise not of one Day, as Stage-players do, the Scene being once past, but the good Will, Admiration, and perpetual Remembrance of their Life to all Posterity, and know that Honours in Heaven are prepared for them? I wish I could express in Words the Representation of that Honour, which in mind I have conceived. Now that I may somewhat propose unto your View the same by some of the first Draughts

and

and Lineaments thereof, confider with your felf, how the brafen Serpent erected by *Mofes* in the Defert of *Arabia*, did heal the Wounds made by other Serpents, by a very Look of the People thereon. Imagine that out of the whole People there were fome ftung by Serpents, and running together for prefent Cure, others Aftonifhed at the newnefs of the Miracle, and all Celebrating with all kind of Praife the immenfe and incredible Goodnefs of God: when they perceive that the Pain of that deadly Wound was not taken away, either by Medicaments, with the Torment of the Patient, by the Phyficians Labour, and affiduous Carefulnefs of Friends, nor by any long fpace of time, but reduced unto Health in a moment. Compare now a King with that Serpent, and fo compare him, that you may reckon a good King amongft the greateft Benefits of God, who alone, without any Expence of thine, and without thy Pains and Labour, doth relieve a Kingdom of all its Troubles, fetleth Perturbations, and in a fhort fpace bringeth the Inveterate Ulcers of Minds unto a Cicatrice or Scar; neither is he only a Procurer of Health to thofe who behold him near at hand, but alfo to fuch as are a far off, and have no hope to fee him, in whofe Image fo great a Force is prefented to the Minds of his Subjects, that it doth eafily perform what the Prudence of Lawyers, the Science of Philofophers, and the Experience of fo many Ages, in collecting their feveral Arts, could never perform. Now that great Honour, Dignity, Eminency or Majefty can be told or excogitate to be in any Man, that by Speech, Converfe, Sight, Fame and a tacite Species prefented to the Mind, he may reduce the moft Luxurious to Modefty, the Violent to Equity, and thofe that are Furious unto a right Mind. Can you ask of God a greater Benefit than this, fo much for the Good of Mans Concerns? If I miftake not, this is the true Reprefentation of a King, not that of a King guarded with Weapons of War, ever fearing others, or making others afraid, by his Hatred towards his People, meafuring his Peoples Hatred againft him. This Reprefentation which we have gived, *Seneca* in his *Thyeftes* hath expreffed in very pleafant Colours, which Verfe I doubt not but you know, feeing it is moft elegant. Do I now feem to fpeak bafely and contemptuoufly of a King, and bind him faft loaded with the Fetters of Laws within a Goal, as you did lately fay? And not rather to bring him forth into Light and Affemblies of Men, and fet him upon the publick Theatre of Mankind? Accompanied not with the arrogant Company of Archers and Armed Men, and Rogues cloathed in Silk, but guarded in Safety by his own Innocency, not with the Terrour of Arms, but by the Love of his People: and not only at Freedom and fet aloft, but

honour-

honoured, venerable, sacred and eminent, and coming forth with the good Wishes and fortunate Acclamations of the People, and whithersoever he goeth, turning the Faces, Eyes and Hearts of all towards him. What Acclamation, or what Triumph can be compared with this daily Pomp? Or if God in humane likeness should come down into Earth, what greater Honour could be given him by Men, than that which would be given to a true King, that is to the lively Image of God? For neither can Love bestow, nor Flattery invent a greater Honour than this. What do you think of this representation of a King?

M. So splendid and magnificent indeed it is, that it seems nothing can be said or imagined more magnificent. But in these corrupt times of ours, it is hard to find this magnanimity, unless careful Education make an honest and good Nature and Disposition. For the mind being principled with good instructions and Acts from Infancy, and by Age and daily Practice confirmed, endeavours by Vertue to attain to true Glory, in vain it is tempted by the allurements of Lusts, or weakned by the impressions of Adversity. For thus Learning doth perfect natural Parts, and good Breeding doth strengthen the mind: So that it findeth occasion of exercising Vertue amongst the very Recreations of Pleasures, and these things which usually terrifie weak ones, by reason of difficulty, Vertue doth account them as a matter of praise. Seeing then there is so great importance in Learning for all conditions of Life, with what great Care and Solicitude should Men foresee, that the tender minds of Kings be rightly principled, even from their very Infancy. For seeing many are the benefits of good Kings towards their Subjects, and contrariwise, many Calamities proceed from wicked Princes, then nothing doth seem to have a greater influence upon every Rank of Men, than the carriage and conversation of Kings and others, who joyntly rule publick Affairs. For what is done well or ill by private Persons, is for the most part hid from the multitude: Or by reason of such Mens obscure condition their example belongeth to few. But all the words and deeds of those, who hold the Helm of publick Affairs, cannot be concealed, being written as it were in a publick Monument, as *Horace* saith, but are set before all Men for imitation. For they do not turn Mens affections to themselves by Studying to please them, but by very kind Allurements of utility. And whithersoever the inclinations of Kings do drive, they make the publick Discipline wheel about with them. But I am afraid that our Kings will not not be intreated to perform what you have now mentioned. For they are so marred by the Allurements of pleasures, and deceived with the false shew of Honour, that I think they do almost that which some

Poets report to have befallen the *Trojans* who were in company at Sea with *Paris*. For the true *Helena* being left in *Ægypt* with *Protheus* a Holy and true religious Man, they did contend so Pertinaciously the space of Ten Years for her likeness, that it was the end of a most pernicious War, and of the most Flourishing Kingdom in those times. For impotent Tyrants embracing that false representation of a Kingdom, when they have once obtained it by right or wrong, cannot loose it without destruction. Now if any do admonish them, that the true *Helena* for whom they imagine to fight, is elsewhere concealed, they would call him mad. *B.* I am indeed glad that you somewhat understand the Beauty of that true Daughter of *Jupiter* from this her likeness, such as it is, albeit you do not see her self. But if these Lovers of that *Helena*, to their great damage, did see the perfect Image of the true *Helena*, pourtracted with her lively Colours by some *Protegenes* or *Apelles*, I do not question but they would admire her and fall in Love with her. And if they did not command their affections to enjoy that other, they might fall into those grievous punishments, which *Persius* in his *Satyres* doth imprecate on Tyrants. O Supream Father of the Gods, be pleased thus to punish cruel Tyrants, when any execrable Lust dipt in raging Poyson doth stir up their spirits, let them see what Vertue is, and let them pine away for sorrow, because they despised her. And therefore seeing we are fallen in to make mention of Tyrants, may it please you, that straight way we proceed to speak of them? *M.* Yea, unless you think some other thing should be first spoken. *B.* I suppose we shall not deviate, if we proceed in the same Foot-steps for finding out a Tyrant, wherein we did insist in seeking out a King. *M.* I think so. For by that means we shall very easily understand what difference there is betwixt them, if set one against another they be duly considered. *B.* And first of all, that we may begin at a Tyrants name, of what Language, it is uncertain. I therefore think it now necessary for us to seek therein the *Greek* or *Latin* Etymology. Now what the Ancients did call Tyranny, I think is not unknown to any who are well versed in humane literature. For Tyrants were called both by the *Greeks* and *Latins*; who had the full Power of all things in their hands, which Power was not astricted by any Bonds of Laws, nor obnoxious to the cognition of Judges. Therefore in both Languages, as you know, not only the Noble Heroes, and most Famous Men, but the chiefest of the Gods, and so *Jupiter* also is called *Tyrannus*: And that even by those who both think and speak Honourably of the Gods. *M.* I know indeed that well enough; and the rather I much admire, whence it is come to pass, that that name now for so many Ages is accounted

The due Priviledge of the Scotch *Government.* 33

counted Odious, and also amongst the most grievous reproaches. *B.* It seems certainly to have fallen out in this word, which happeneth to be in many others; for if you consider the nature of Words, it hath no evil in it. And albeit some words have a more pleasant sound in the Ears of Hearers, and others a more unpleasant, yet of themselves they have no such thing, so as to stir up the mind to Wrath, Hatred, or Hilarity, or otherwise to Create pleasure or pain and trouble. If any such thing befal us, that happens to fall out usually, not from the Word, but from the consuetude of Men, and Image thereof conceived by the Hearers. Therefore a Word which amongst some Men is honest, amongst others cannot be heard with some Preface of, *with reverence.* M. I remember that the like is befallen the names of *Nero* and *Judas*, whereof the one amongst the *Romans*, and the other amongst the *Jews* was accounted by great Men very Famous and honourable. But thereafter by no fault of these names, but of these two Men, it hath come to pass, that even the most flagitious Men will not have these names to be given their Children: They being Buried under such infamy. *B.* The same also is perspicuous to have befallen the Word *Tyrant*, for it is credible, that the first Magistrates, who were thus called, were good Men; or from hence, that this name was sometime so Honourable, that it was attributed to the Gods. But those that came afterwards made it so infamous by their wicked Deeds, that all Men abhorred it as Contagious and Pestilentious, and thought it a more light reproach to be called an Hangman than a Tyrant. *M.* Perhaps it was the same as befell the Kings in *Rome* after the *Tarquinii* were deposed in the name *Dictator* after M. *Antonius* and P. *Dolabella* were Consuls. *B.* Just so. And on the contrary, base and vulgar names have been made Famous by the Vertue of Men called thereby. As amongst the *Romans, Camillus, Metellus, Scropha* ; and amongst the *Germans, Henry, Genserick, Charles.* This you shall the better understand, if taking away the name of Tyrant, you consider the thing, notwithstanding that this kind of Government hath continued in its former Honour and Respect amongst many Famous Nations, as the *Æsymnetæ* amongst the *Grecians*, and the *Dictators* amongst the *Romans:* For both were lawful Tyrants. Now Tyrants they were, being more powerful than the Laws; but lawful they were, as being chosen by consent of the People. *M.* What am I hearing? Tyrants and yet lawful? Indeed I did expect a far other thing from you; but now you seem to confound the differences of all Kings and Tyrants. *B.* Indeed both Kings and Tyrants amongst the Ancients seem to have been altogether one and the same, but I suppose in divers Ages: For I think the name of Tyrants was more Ancient;

F 2 there-

thereafter when they became weary of the name, in their place succeeded Kings by a more plausible name, and more gentle Government; and when they also began to degenerate, the moderation of Laws were adhibited, which might set limits to the boundless Lusts of their Government. Now Men according to the exigence of times, and their usual way, seeking out New Remedies became weary of the Old way of Government, and sought out New ways. Now our present purpose is to handle both kinds of Government, namely that wherein as well the Government of Kings as of Laws is the most powerful; and the worst kind of Tyranny, wherein all things are contrary to a Kingdom, and have undertaken to compare them one with another. *M.* It is so. And I earnestly expect you would fall upon that. *B.* At first then we had agreed, that a King was Created for maitaining humane Society, and we determined his Office and Duty, that by the prescript of Laws he should allow every Man his own. *M.* I do remember that. *B.* First then, he that doth not receive a Government by the will of the People, but by force Invadeth it, or intercepteth it by fraud, how shall we call him? *M.* I suppose, a Tyrant. *B.* There be also many other differences, which I shall briefly run through, because any Man may easily Collect them from *Aristotle*: For the Government of Kings is according to Nature, but that of Tyrants is not. A King doth Rule his Subjects, and Reign over them by their own Consent. Tyrants Reign over them, nill they will they. A Kingdom is a principality of a Free Man among Free Men: Tyranny is a principality of a Master over his Slaves. For defence of a Kings safety the Subjects Watch and Ward, for a Tyrant Forrainers do Watch to oppress the Subjects. The one beareth Rule for the Subjects well-fare, the other for himself. *M.* What do you say of those who have gotten into their hand the Supream Authority by Force and without the Peoples Consent, and yet for many Years did so Rule, that the People were not weary of their Government? For what could be wanting in *Hiero* the *Syracusan* King, or in *Cosmo de Medices* the *Florentine* Duke to make them just Kings, except the Peoples suffrages? *B.* Indeed we cannot exempt them out of the number of Tyrants. For it was Nobly spoken by a notable Historian, albeit you may indeed Rule your Country and Friends by Violence and Force, and Correct their Faults, yet it is unseasonable. Then again, such do seem to do just like Robbers, who cunningly dividing their ill gotten Goods, do seek the praise of Justice by injury, and of liberality by Robbery, yet do not obtain what they hunt for; by the odiousness of one ill deed they loose all the thanks of their Ostentative bounty, and so much the less assurance of their Civil disposition do they give their Subjects,

jects, and that becaufe they do not that for their Subjects good, but for their own Government, namely, that they the more fecurely may enjoy their own Lufts and Pleafures, and eftablifh a foveraignty over the Pofterity to come, having fomewhat mitigated the Peoples hatred. Which when they have once done, they turn back again to their old manners. For the fruit which is to follow may eafily be known by the fowre thereof. For he hath the fame ftrength and power to revoke all things at his pleafure, and to transfer unto himfelf the ftrength of all Laws, even as if he would abrogate all Laws. But this kind of Tyrants had been perhaps tolerable, if without the common deftruction of all it could have been taken away, even as we do endure fome bodily Difeafes, rather than throw our life into the hazard of a doubtfome Cure. But they who bear rule, not for their Country's good, but for their own felf interefts, have no regard to the publick utility, but to their own pleafure and luft, they place the ftability of their Authority in the Peoples weaknefs, and think that a Kingdom is not a procuration concredited to them by God, but rather a prey put into their hands. Such are not joyned to us by any civil Bond, or Bond of humanity, but fhould be accounted the greateft Enemies of God and of all Men. For all the actions of Kings fhould aim at the publick fafety of their Subjects, and not at their own wealth. By how much Kings are raifed above other Men, fo much fhould they imitate the Celeftial Bodies, which having no good offices of ours given to them; yet do infufe on human Affairs a vital and bountiful vertue of heat and light. Yea the very Titles wherewith we have honoured Kings (if you remember) might put them in mind of their Munificence. *M.* Me thinks I remember, namely that they fhould ufe a Paternal indulgence towards their Subjects committed to them as towards Children; the care of a Shepherd in procuring their profit; as Generals in maintaining their fafety, as Governours in excellency of Vertues, and as Emperours commanding thofe things which might be ufeful. *B.* Can he then be called a Father who accounts his Subjects Slaves? or a Shepherd, who doth not feed his Flock, but devoureth them? or a Pilot who doth always ftudy to make fhipwrack of the goods in his Ship, and who as (they fay) makes a Leek in the very Ship wherein he fails? *M.* By no means. *B.* What is he then, who doth not Rule for the Peoples good, but ftill doth all for himfelf, who doth not ftrive with good Men in Vertue, but contendeth to exceed the moft flagitious wretch in Vices? who leadeth his Subjects into manifeft Snares? *M.* Indeed fuch fhall not by me be accounted either a General, or Emperour, or Governour. *B.* If you then fhall fee any ufurping the

name

name of a King, and in no kind of Vertue excelling any of the People but inferior to many therein, not fatherly affectionate towards his Subjects, but rather oppressing them by arrogant domineering, and that thinketh the People is concredited to him for his own gain, and not for their safeguard. Will you imagine that such a Man is truely a King, albeit he goes vapouring with a great many in Guard about him, and openly be seen with gorgeous Apparel, and make a shew of Punishments? can he conciliate the People, and catch their applause by Rewards, Games, Pompous shews, and even mad underminings, and whatever is thought to be Magnificent? will you, I say, account such a Man a King? *M.* Not indeed, If I would understand my self aright, but void of all human society. *B.* Within what limits do you circumscribe human society? *M.* Within the very same limits wherein by your preceding discourse you seemed to include it, namely within the Hedg of Laws. Which whosoever trangress, be they Robbers, Thieves, or Adulterers, I see them publickly punished, and that to be accounted a just cause of their Punishment, because they transgressed the limits of human society. *B.* What say you of those, who would never once enter within these hedges? *M.* I think they should be accounted Enemies to God and Men, and reckoned amongst Wolves, or some other kind of noisome Beasts, rather than amongst Men: which whosoever doth nourish, he nourisheth them for his own destruction and others: and whosoever killeth them, doth not only good to himself, but to all others. But if I had power to make a Law, I would command (which the *Romans* were wont to do with Monsters) such kind of Men to be carried away into solatary places, or to be drowned in the depths of the Sea, a far from the sight of any Land, left by the Contagion of their Carcasses they might infect other Men. And rewards to the killers of them to be discerned not only by the whole People, but by every particular Person; as useth to be done to those who have killed Wolves or Bears, or apprehended their Whelps. For if such a Monster should be Born, and speak with a Mans voice, and have the Face of a Man, and likeness of other Parts, I would have no fellowship with him; or if any Man devested of humanity should degenerate into such cruelty, as he would not meet with other Men but for their destruction. I think he should be called a Man no more than Satyrs, Apes, or Bears, albeit they should resemble Man in countenance, gesture and speech. *B.* Now if I mistake not, you understand what a King, and what a Tyrant the wisest Antients meant in their Writings. Will it please you then that we propose some Idea of a Tyrant also, such as we gave in speaking of a King? *M.* Yes, that I do do earneſtly deſire, if it be not a trouble to you. *B*. You have not forgot, I ſuppoſe, what by the Poets is ſpoken of the Furies, and by our Divines of the Nature of evil ſpirits, namely, that theſe ſpirits are Enemies of Mankind, who whilſt they are in perpetual Torments, yet do rejoyce in the Torments of Men. This is indeed the true Idea of Tyranny. But becauſe this Idea can only be diſcerned in the imagination, but not by any of the ſenſes, I ſhall ſet before you another Idea, which not only the Mind may diſcern, but the ſenſes alſo perceive, and as it were repreſented to the very Eye. Imagine you ſee a Ship toſſed by Waves in the Sea, and all the Shoars round about not only without Haven or Harbour, but alſo full of moſt cruel Enemies, and the Maſter of the Ship in conteſt with the Company, and yet to have no other hope of ſafety than in their fidelity, and the ſame not certain, as knowing well that he puts his life into the Hands of a moſt barbarous kind of Men, and void of all humanity, whom by Money he may hold truſty, and who for greater gain may be conduced to fight againſt him. Such indeed is that life which Tyrants embrace as happy. They are afraid of Enemies abroad, and of their Subjects at home, and not only of their Subjects, but of their Domeſticks, Kinsfolks, Brethren, Wives, Children and near Relations. And therefore they have always War, either a Foreign War with their Neigbours, Civil War with their Subjects, or a Domeſtick War within doors, or elſe they are ſtill in fear thereof. Neither do they expect aid any where but by a Mercenary way, they dare not hire good Men, nor can they truſt bad Men; what then in all their life can be to them pleaſant? *Dionyſius* would not let his Daughters once become Women to trim him, fearing to let the Razor come to his Throat. *Temoleon* was killed by his own Brother, *Alexander Pharaus* by his own Wife, and *Sp. Caſſias* by his own Father. He that ſtill hath ſuch Examples ſet before his Eyes, what a Torture do you imagine he carrieth about in his Breaſt? Seeing he thinks that he is the mark ſet for all Mankind to ſhoot at. Neither is he only, while awake, tormented with theſe tortures of Conſcience, but alſo is awakned out of his Sleep by terrifying ſights both of living and dead, and agitated by the Firebrands of helliſh Furies. For the ſeaſon which Nature doth grant for reſt to all Creatures, and alſo to Men for relaxation of their Cares, to him is turned into horrours and puniſhment. *M.* Forſooth you have handled theſe things very acutely, but I know not if truly alſo, but yet, if I miſtake not, they make not ſo much for our purpoſe.

For

For they who have the power to choose what Kings they please, in them is the power to bind by Laws such as they have chosen. But you know that our Kings are not chosen, but born Kings. To whom I have always thought it to be no less hereditary, that their will and pleasure should stand for Law, than the Kingdom it self. Nor am I rashly induced to be of this opinion, but convinced by several great Authors, with whom I am not ashamed to be mistaken, (if at all I be in any mistake or errour.) For not to make mention of others, Lawyers do affirm, that by the Royal Law which is made for the Government of Kings, all the Peoples Power is so transmitted into them, that their will and pleasure should be accounted for Laws. And indeed from this Law did those threatnings of a certain Emperour arise, that he would quite take away from Lawyers all their sciences, wherein they so much boast, by one Edict. *B.* You do very well, that whilst you cite a most wicked Author of one of the greatest deeds, thought good to suppress his name. For that was *C. Caligula,* who wished but one Neck for all the people of *Rome.* Now in that Emperour there was nothing of a man, far less of a King, beside his shape, you are not then ignorant how much Authority may be due to him. But as for the Royal Law, what it is, when, by whom, and in what words it was made the very Lawyers make no mention. For that power was never in any of the Roman Emperours, seeing from them appeals were made to the people. But that ordinance, whereby *L. Flaccus* having oppressed the Liberty of the People of *Rome,* established by the silence of other Laws ; the Tyranny of *L. Sylla,* no man did ever hold for a Law. For of that ordinance such was the strength, that whatever *L. Sylla* had done, should be ratified. Which Law never any free people was so infatuate, as willingly to permit to be imposed on them. Or if any such were, he were indeed worthy to serve perpetually Tyrants, and be punished for his folly. But if any such Law have been, let us think it was an example proposed to us for caution, but not for imitation.

M. Indeed you admonish well. But that admonition belongeth to them in whose power it is to create such Kings as most please them, but to us it doth not at all belong, who do not by suffrages elect the best Kings, but accept of those that by chance are given us. That also of a certain Lawyer seems properly to quadrate with us, who have given to our Kings *Ancestors* that right and authority over us and our posterity, that they and their posterity

The due Priviledge of the Scotch *Government.*

rity should perpetually hold their Empire and Authority over us. I wish then you had admonished them (I mean our *Ancestors*) who once had it in their own power entirely to admit such Kings as they pleased. But now that Counsel of yours too late serves only for this, not to amend the faults that are not in our power, but deplore our *Ancestors* folly, and acknowledge the misery of our condition. For what can be left to those that are made slaves, but to be punished for other mens folly? And that our punishment may be made more light, let us asswage them by patience: let us not provoke their wrath, by tumultuating importunely, whose dominion over us we cannot cast off, nor diminish their power, nor flee from their force or weakness. Now that Royal Law, to which you are so much an Adversary, was not made in favour of Tyrants, as you would have it seem to be, because it was approved by *Justinian* a very just Prince. With whom so plain flattery would not have had place. For with a foolish Prince that of the Poet would prevail *whom do th false honour help, or lying infamy terrify, but a lewd man and a lyar?* B. Indeed *Justinian*, as History reports, was a great mighty Man albeit some do report him to have been cruelly ingrate to *Bellisarius.* But let him be such as you judge he was, yet you may remember, that it is recorded by some almost of that same age with him, that *Tribonius*, a chief Man amongst the compilers of these Laws, was a very wicked Man, and so might easily be induced to gratify also a very bad Prince. But even good Princes do not hate this kind of flattery. For *Even those who will not kill any man, do yet desire to have it in their power, and there is nothing which he dare not believe of himself, seeing his power equal to that of the Gods is commended.* But let us return to our own Princes: to whom you say the Kingdom doth come by inheritance and not by suffrages. Now of our own only I speak, for if I shall digress to speak of Foreign Princes, I fear left our discourse become more prolixe than we intended. *M.* I think you should do so. For Foreign Affairs do not much belong to our dispute in hand. B. That I may therefore begin at the first Principles. This is sufficiently agreed upon, that our Princes were chosen for their Vertue, who should govern others. *M.* So do the Writers of our Affairs record. B. Nor is this less known, that many who have Reigned cruelly and wickedly have been called to account by their Subjects: some adjudged to perpetual Imprisonment, others punished partly by exile, and partly by death, against whose killers no Inquisition was ever made.

made, even when their Sons or Kinsmen were assumed into their stead. But who ever had killed good Kings, were more severely punished, so as no where else was murther more severely revenged. And because it would be tedious to rehearse every one, I shall produce some few of these last Kings, whose memory is most recent. The nobility did so grievously punish the Murther of *James* the First, (having left as heir his Son of six years of age) that by a new and exquisit kind of punishment they put to death several Persons of very Eminent Families, and Peers of the Land, both for wealth and vassalage eminent: On the contrary, who did condole the death of *James* the Third, a Man flagitious and cruel? far less revenge it? But in the death of *James* the Fourth his Son, the suspition of the Crime was punished with death neither were our Ancestors piously inclined towards good Kings, but also gentle and merciful toward wicked Kings. For when one of King *Culen's* Enemies had killed him in his journey, whilst he is coming to give an account of his Administration, he was severely punished by a sentence of the Estates of Parliament. And likewise was punished as an Enemy, he who had killed *Evenus* in Prison, who had been adjudged to perpetual bonds. And the violent death or parricide of him they punished, whose wicked and vicious life all men had hated. *M.* I do not so much inquire at present what some time hath been done, as by what right Kings Reign amongst us. *B.* That we may therefore return thereunto, as in our first Kings until *Kenneth* the Third, who first setled the Kingdom in his own Family, it is very clear what was the peoples power in creating their Kings, and taking order with them, even so it is necessary we know, that he either did that against the peoples will, or by perswasion obtained it. *M.* That cannot be denied. *B.* Moreover, If by force he compelled the people to obey him, then how soon the people began to have confidence in their own strength, they might have cast off that violent yoke of Government imposed upon them: Seeing all Laws received by Kings and People do pronounce, and nature it self doth call for it, that whatever is done by force and violence, may be undone by the like violence. *M.* What if the people being by fraud circumvented, or by fear forced did surrender themselves into that Slavery: what for excuse can be pretended, but that they perpetually continue in that case, into which it was once agreed they were to be in? *B.* If you debate with me from that agreement, what excuse there is for undoing the same. I shall on the other hand lay down some reasons why pactions and agreements

greements may be diffolved. And firft of all, fuch as are made through force or fear, in all Common-wealths, concerning thefe there is a fure Law, drawn from Natures fpring. Laws allow reftitution to be fully made to fuch as are by fraud circumvented, and think that it fhould be kept for Pupils, and fuch other Perfons, who by juft Law they would have to be defended. What Affembly therefore of Men can require more juftly to have reftitution, then a whole people? to whom the wrong is done, which indeed is not done againft one part of the Common-wealth, but floweth far abroad into all the Members of that politick Body. *M.* I know this Law to be made ufe of in the cafes of private Perfons, nor is it unjuft. But there is no neceffity we fhould debate herein, feeing it is far more credible (which is recorded by Hiftorians) that that right was by the peoples will granted to Kings. *B.* It is alfo credible that fo great a matter was not obtained without fome great caufe. *M.* I do eafily affent thereto. *B.* What do you think was the chief caufe thereof? *M.* What other, except that which is recorded? wearifomnefs of ambition, Tumults, Murthers, inteftine Wars, often with the utter deftruction of the one party, and always with very great damage of both. For fuch as did obtain the Government, endeavoured to cut off their Brethren, and almoft all their near Kinfmen, that they might leave the Government the more peaceable to their Children, even as we hear is done amongft the *Turks*, and as we fee amongft the chief of the Clanns in our *Iflands*, and in *Ireland*. *B.* To which of the two do you think was that contention moft pernicious, to the People or to the Princes? *M.* Certainly to the Kings, feeing the greateft part of the people fecuring themfelves doth ufually ftand Spectators of Princes contefts, and yield always as a prey to the Victors. *B.* It feems then that Princes rather for themfelves, than for the good of the people defired to eftablifh the Kingdom in their own Family. *M.* That is very probable. *B.* Now that they might obtain that which did fo much concern the perpetual dignity, wealth and fafety of their Family, it is probable, that they did difpenfe or remit to one another fomewhat of their right: and that they might the more eafily obtain the peoples good will, liking and confent, they on their part gave them fome eafe. *M.* I believe that. *B.* You will certainly confefs it incredible, that for fo great a benefit beftowed on their Kings, they fhould endure to be in a worfe cafe than formerly they were in. *M.* It is altogether incredible. *B.* Neither would Kings have defired

fired it with fo great Ambition, if they had known it would prove hurtful to their Children, and unprofitable to the people. *M.* Not at all. *B.* Imagine then that some one in Parliament of the free people did freely ask the King, what if to any King should succeed a Son that is a fool, or mad? Will you let such over us to Rule us, who cannot rule or govern themselves? *M.* I think there was no need to make use of that exception, seeing by the Laws it is provided against such a case. *B.* Well said indeed. Let us then see, if Kings had obtained from the people a free power over the Laws, whether that had been unprofitable, especially to those who desired to foresee the good of their own Family in time coming. *M.* Why shall we think that that Power would be unprofitable? *B.* Because nothing doth so much contribute for the continuance of a Government, as that temperament of Government, seeing it is both honourable for Kings, and moderate, and safe for the people. The mind of Man hath somewhat sublime and generous imbred therein by nature, that it will obey none, unless he govern profitably: Nor is there any thing more prevalent for maintaining humane society, than the mutual exchange of benefits, and therefore *Theopompus* seems to have wisely answered his Wife upbraiding him that by adding the *Ephory* he had diminished the Power of his Authority, and had left the Kingdom to his Sons less than he had gotten it. It is, faith he, so much the more firm and sure. *M.* What you relate of continuance, I perceive is most true. For I think the Kingdoms of the *Scots* and *Danes* are the most Ancient of all that are in *Europe*, nor do they seem by any other means to have attain'd that antiquity, than by the moderation of the Supream Authority, whilst in the mean time the Kingdoms of the *Frenches*, *Englishes* and *Spaniards* have past so often out of one Family into another. But I do not know if our Kings have been so wise as *Theopompus*. *B.* As they have not been so prudent, do you imagine that the people were so foolish, as to neglect an occasion so opportune put into their hand? or that they were so struck with fear, or seduced by flatteries, as to give themselves over into slavery willingly? *M.* Perhaps it was not. But if the people (which indeed might be) were so blind, that they did not see what might concern their own good, or being careless would not see what might be for their benefit, so as to contemn it, should they not then be justly punished for their folly? *B.* It is not probable, that any such thing was done, seeing we may see the contrary to

be

be observed even to our days. For besides that wicked Kings, as often as they intended Tyranny over their Subjects, were always restrained, some Vestiges of the Ancient Customs do yet continue in some Ancient Families. For the Old Scots even to our very days do choose their Heads of Clans, and having chosen them, do give them a Council of Elders, to which Council whosoever gives not Obedience, is deprived of all Honour and Dignity. What therefore is with very great care observed in the parts, would they be negligent of for the security and safety of all? And would they willingly redact themselves into Bondage to him, who was to possess a lawful Kingdom instead of some benefit? and would they freely give over their Liberty acquired by vertue, defended by arms, not interrupted for so many Ages, to one not expecting it, without force, without War? For the calamity of *John Baliol* doth shew that that power was never granted to our Kings, besides the punishments so often taken for their Male-administration. Who about two hundred and sixty years ago was by the Nobility rejected, because he had subjected himself and his Kingdom to the authority of *Edward* King of *England*, and *Robert* the first was substitute in his stead. The same doth also shew that perpetual Custom continued from the beginning of our Government.

M. What custom do you speak of? *B.* When our Kings are publickly inaugurated, they solemnly promise to all the people, that they will observe the Laws, Rites and old Statutes of their predecessors and use the same power which they have received from them, that whole order of ceremonies doth shew, and the first entry of our Kings into every City, from all which it may be easily understood, what kind of power they did receive from our predecessors, to wit, none other than that they swear to maintain the Laws being chosen by suffrages. This condition of reigning did God propose to *David*, and his posterity, and promiseth they should reign so long, as they should obey the Laws he had given them, those things indeed they do, as is probable that our Kings received from our Ancestors a power not immense, but within certain limits bounded and limited. And further there was the confirmation of a long time, and the usurpation of a perpetual right by the people, never reprehended by a publick decree. *M.* But I fear it cannot be easily obtained of Kings as being perswaded by that probability to condescend to these Laws however sworn unto, or usurped by the people. *B.* I also believe, it is no less hard to perswade the people to pass

from

from the right received from their Anceſtors, approved by the uſe of ſo many ages, and practiſed by one continual tenour. I do not think it needful to proceed by conjectures what the people is to do, ſince I ſee what they have done already. But if by the obſtinate pertinacy of both the buſineſs they come to Arms, he that prevaileth will give what Law and right he pleaſeth to the vanquiſhed: but this will no longer continue than he who is vanquiſhed, having again gathered together his forces, ſhall take up Arms again. In all which contentions men uſually ſtill fight with very great damage of the people, but with the utter overthrow of Kings. For from this Spring do flow all the deſtructions of all Kingdoms. *M.* It muſt needs be ſo. *B.* I have perhaps gone back further than was needful, to the end you might clearly underſtand what kind of Government there was amongſt us of old. For if I had reaſoned with you according to the rigour of the Law, I might have gained my point in a far more compendious way. *M.* Albeit you have almoſt ſatisfied me already, yet I ſhall willingly hear what that is. *B.* I would then have you firſt of all to anſwer me this queſtion. Do you not approve the definition of Law ſet down by Lawyers, who ſay that Law is, that which the people knew when demanded by him to whom the Prerogative of demanding belongeth. *M.* Indeed I do approve it. *B.* We have agreed, that the faults of Laws being found out, they may be amended or abrogated by the Law-givers. *M.* We did ſo. *B.* I ſuppoſe you perceive now, that ſuch as are born Kings are by the Laws and ſuffrages of the people created, no leſs than thoſe whom we ſaid were elected in the beginning, and that in receiving of Laws there will not be Remedies wanting in the people, who are the Lawgivers, not only againſt force and fraud, but alſo againſt negligence. *M.* I perceive that clearly. *B.* Only here is the difference, that the Law concerning our Kings was made ſeveral ages before, and when any doth enter into the Kingdom, there uſeth to be no new Law made, but the old Law is approved, and ratified. But amongſt thoſe who have their meeting of Eſtates at the Election of every King, the Law uſeth to be made, the King created and approved, and ſo to enter into his Government. *M.* It is ſo. *B.* Now if you pleaſe, let us briefly recapitulate what we are at accord in from the very beginning. So that if ought be raſhly approved, it may be retracted. *M.* I am content. *B.* Firſt of all then, it ſeems that a King is created for the Peoples ſake, and

and that nothing more excellent is given us of God than a good King, and more Peſtilentious than a wicked King. *M.* Very right. *B.* We have alſo ſaid that a wicked King is called a Tyrant. *M.* We have ſaid ſo. *B.* And becauſe there is not ſuch plenty of good men, ſo as to chooſe thoſe who may prove good Kings, nor ſo great a happineſs of Birth, as that good Luck may offer us thoſe that are good: if we have not ſuch as we would wiſh, yet we have ſuch as either conſent hath approved, or chance hath offered. Now the hazard that occureth either in chooſing new Kings, or in approving ſuch as are given us by Birth, was the cauſe that we deſired Laws, which might modify the Government of Kings. Now theſe Laws ſhould be nothing elſe but the expreſs Image (as far as may be) of a good Prince. *M.* We are at accord in that alſo. *B.* It now remaineth, as I ſuppoſe, for us to ſpeak of the Puniſhment of Tyrants. *M.* That only ſeems to remain unſpoken of. *B.* If then a King break all the Bonds of Laws, and plainly behave himſelf as a publick Enemy, what think you ſhould be done in this caſe? *M.* Indeed I am at a ſtand here. For albeit the reaſons you have given ſeem to convince me, that we ought to have no ſociety with that King, yet ſo great is the ſtrength of a conſtant cuſtom that in my opinion it hath the ſtrength of a Law. Which cuſtom doth ſo cloſely cleave to men in their minds, that if at any time it hath brought in an errour, better it is to tolerate it, than to marr the Conſtitution of the whole Body, whilſt we endeavour to Cure a Diſeaſe that is but ſmall by cuſtom. For ſuch is the Nature of ſome diſeaſes, that better it is to endure the Pain they bring, than to call for doubtſom remedies, in the applying whereof, albeit the Cure may be wrought, yet they bring ſuch ſharp Pains in their Cure, as that the Cure of the Diſeaſe is more pernicious than the Diſeaſe it ſelf. Next, that which troubles me more is, I ſee that Government which you call Tyranny, confirmed by the Word of God, and what you abhorr as the utter overthrow of Laws, God doth call the Law of the Kingdom; the Authority of that paſſage of Scripture doth move me more than all the Arguments of Philoſophers. If you do not explain this to me, the comments of Men will not be of ſo great account with me, but that I may inſtantly fall away to the Adverſaries ſide. *B.* You are, as I perceive, in the common errour, and that very grievous, who do endeavour to confirm Tyranny by Tyranny. For how great the Tyranny of cuſtom is in the minds of men, wherein

wherein it hath taken deepest root, and too often we have found it in this our age. *Herodotus* an Ancient writer doth give us warning by an old example, but I need not old examples. Be well advised. Consider with your self how many things there be of great moment, wherein you following the dictates of reason have fallen from a custom inveterat so many ages past, so that now you might have learned by Domestick experiments, that there is no custom more full of dangers than that which in a publick way they command us to follow. I bid you look well to it round about, how many ruins, and how great slaughters will you see therein? but if it be more clear (as we say) then the very light, I need not tarry longer in proving or Illustrating a thing so perspicuous. Now as for that passage of Scripture, which from the History of the Kings you rather signify than explain, beware, I pray you, you think that the things which God doth abhor in the life of Tyrants, are by him allowed to Kings. Now left this be, I bid you first consider what that people sought of the Lord: then what causes of a new petition they had, lastly, what the Lord did answer them. First, they ask a King, but what a King? a Lawful King? such a one they had. For *Samuel* was given them by the Lord, whose Prerogative it was to set a King over them. He had for many years judged them Lawfully according to prescript of God's Law: but whilst in his old Age his Sons did judge, they did many things wickedly, and judged contrary to the Laws. I see no reason why they should ask the change, or rather Amendment of the Government, or expect the same from the Lord, who not long before had quite rooted out the whole Family of *Heli*, almost for the like cause. What do they ask? A King, such as their Neighbouring Nations had, who at home might be a judge to them, and abroad a leader of their Armies. Now in effect such were Tyrants, for as the People of *Asia* are of a more servile disposition than those of *Europe*, so did they the more easily obey the commands of Tyrants. There is no mention made for ought I know, by an Historian of any Lawful King in *Asia*. Moreover, it doth easily appear that a Tyrant, and not a King is there described, in regard the Lord in Deuteronomy had prescribed to them a form not only different from this in that place cited by you, but also plainly contrary thereto, according to which form *Samuel* and the other judges had judged so many years, which whilst they did reject, the Lord complains, that he was by them rejected. *M.* But the Lord doth not call him Tyrant,

rant, but ever King. *B.* He calls him indeed King: for it is peculiar to the Lord, to use the common Speech of the People, as often as he speaketh to a people. And therefore he maketh use of that word with the Vulgar People: but left an Ambiguous use thereof might deceive, he doth Eloquently expound what the use of that word was amongst Neighbouring Nations. *M.* As that may be true, yet that of the Apostle *Paul* doth urge us more narrowly, who commands us to pray for the safety of Princes: he is so far from permitting us to revile Government, much less to dethrone such as are invested therewith, or to kill them being thrown down. But what Princes doth he recommend to our Prayers? the most cruel that ever were, *Tiberius, Caligula, Claudius, Nero.* For *Pauls* Epistles were almost contemporary with them. *B.* That you make so much account of the Authority in *Paul,* so as one Sentence of his hath more weight with you than the writings of all Philosophers and Lawyers, I think you do well: but see that you consider well his judgment, or meaning: for you must not examin the words only, but in what time, to whom, and why he wrote. First then let us see what *Paul* did write. For he writeth to *Titus.* Chap. 3. Put them in mind to be Subject to Principalities and powers, and to be ready to every good work. I suppose, you see what end of obedience and subjection he appoints. He likewise to Timothy Chap. 2. Doth write, that we should pray for all men, even for Kings, and other Magistrates, that saith he, we may live a peaceable life in all Godliness and honesty. And here you see what end of praying he appoints: namely not for the Kings safety, but the Churches Tranquillity, from which it will be no difficult thing to conceive also the form of Prayer. Now in his Epistle to the *Romans,* he doth define a King near to a Logick subtilty, for saith he, he is a Minister to whom the sword is given by God, for punishing the wicked, and for cherishing and relieving the good. For saith *Chrisostome,* these things are not by *Paul* written of a Tyrant, but of a true and Lawful Magistrate, who is the Vice-gerent of the true God on Earth, whom whosoever resisteth, doth certainly resist the ordinance of God. Now albeit we ought to pray for wicked Princes, we should not thence conclude, that their vices should not be punished: nor will it more follow that we should not punish the rapines of *Robbers,* for whom we are also commanded to Pray: And if we should obey a good Prince, it will not therefore follow that we should **not** resist a wicked Prince. But if you consider the reason which did move *Paul* to write these things, look that the place or Argument make not much against you. For he wrote this to chastise the rashness of some, who did deny the Authority of Magistrates to be necessary for *Christians*. For since the power of Magistrats is ordained against wicked men, that we may all live rightously; and an example of Divine Justice might remain amongst men, they affirmed that there was no use thereof amongst men, who abhor so much the contagion of vices, as that they are a Law to themselves. *Paul* doth not therefore speak of those who bear Rule as Magistrats, but of Magistracy it self, that is, of the function and office of those who rule: nor yet of one or other kind of Magistracy, but of every form of a Lawful Magistracy. Nor doth he debate with those who think that wicked Magistrates should be restrained, but with those men who deny all Authority of Magistrates, who absurdly interpreting *Christian* liberty, did affirm it to be an indignity for those that were made free by the Son of God, and ruled by the Spirit of God, to be under the power of any man. That *Paul* might refute their errour, he sheweth, that Magistracy is a thing not only good, but also sacred, namely an ordinance of God, and for that end instituted, that the assemblies and incorporations of men might be so continued, that they might acknowledge Gods benefits towards them, and might forbear to wrong one another. God commanded them to be keepers of his Laws who were constituted in dignity. Now if we confess Laws to be good (as indeed they are) and the keepers thereof worthy of Honour, we will be forced to confess that the office of the keepers is a good and profitable thing. But Magistracy is terrible, but to whom? to the good, or bad? to the good it is not a terrour: it being to them a defence from injury: but to wicked men it is a terrour: it is not so to you, who are ruled by the Spirit of God. But you will say to me, what need have I then to be Subject to Magistracy, if I be the Lords Freeman? yea, that you may approve your self to be the Lords Freeman, obey his Laws: for the Spirit of the Lord, by whom you boast to be led and governed, is both the Law-giver, and approver of Magistrates, and also the Author of obedience to Magistrates. We therefore in this will easily agree together, that there is need of Magistracy even in the best Common-wealths, and that we should every way honour the same. But if any man think otherwise, we account him mad, infamous and worthy of all Punishment. For he doth plainly contravene the will of God

revealed

The due Priviledge of the Scotch Government. 49

revealed to us in the Scriptures. But as for *Caligula*, *Nero*, *Domitian*, and such like Tyrants, why they should not be punished as breakers of divine and humane Law, you have nothing here from *Paul*, who treats of the power of Magistrates, but not of the wicked Ministers of that power, nor will they be at all Magistrates, if you examine that kind of Tyrants according to *Pauls* rule. But if any will debate that wicked Princes are also ordained by God, look that this his discourse be not captious. For (as they say in Proverb) God may put a hard wedge to cleave a hard knot, so doth he set up a wicked man for punishing of wicked men; but no man in his right wits dare affirm, that God is therefore the Author of evil, or wickedness, even as no man is Ignorant that he is the Author of punishing wicked men. A good Magistrates also for the most part chooseth a wicked man to be an hangman for punishing guilty Persons. And albeit indeed that a Magistrate doth assume such an hangman for that Office, yet no impunity is granted him of all his misdeeds. Nor will the Magistrate have him to be so above the Laws, as that he cannot be questioned thereby. I will not stay longer upon this similitude, lest Court flatterers cry out that I speak basely of the supream Magistrate. But however they exclaim, certainly this they cannot deny, that the hangmans function is a part of the publick Office, and perhaps of the Royal Office, or at least by the Testimony of very Kings; who complain that their Majesty and Person is wronged, as oft as any of their publick Ministers is wronged, or violence done to them: Now the punishment of wicked Malefactors, and whatever else of that kind, doth belong to the Kings office. What say you of Majors or Provosts in Towns? what of Generals of Armies? what of Baillies? What of Sherifs? doth not *Paul* command us to be subject to them? doth he hold them for private persons? Now an account useth to be taken for male-administration of all, not only of Inferiour Magistrates, but also of such as are equal to Kings. I would therefore have them, who from *Pauls* words do dream that so great a power is given to Kings, to shew me from him, that Kings only are here to be understood by the name of power, and therefore they only are to be exempted from the Punishment of Laws: or if, when we say powers, other Magistrates be also understood by the same Author, who are ordained by God for the same use: I would have them also to shew me, where all Magistrates are loosed from the Laws, and pronounced free from the fear of Punish-

H 2 ment:

ment: or if this immunity be granted to Kings only, but denyed to others who are set in Authority. *M.* But *Paul* will have all to be subject to the higher powers. *B.* He commandeth so indeed, but by this name of Power he must needs comprehend other Magistrates, unless perhaps we imagin that *Paul* doth think no Power at all to be in those Common-wealths, which have not Kingly Government, but plainly an Anarchy therein. *M.* I do not believe that, nor is it probable: and the rather I am of this opinion, because the current of all the most learned Interpreters on the place make for you: who think that *Paul's* dispute there was against those that affirmed that no Laws and Magistrates did at all belong to them. *B.* What say you to that which I lately spoke. Do you think, that those Tyrants before mentioned of all men the most cruel, are meant by the Apostle?

M. Yes, but what produce you against me to hinder me from the belief thereof? especially seing *Jeremy* doth earnestly advise the *Jews*, and that by command of God, to obey the King of *Assyria*, and by no means to reject his autority, and thence they infer by the like reason, that obedience should be given to other Tyrants also how cruel soever. *B.* That I may answer first to what you last spoke you must take notice, that the Prophet doth not command the *Jews* to obey all Tyrants, but the King of *Assyria* alone: Now if you would conclude the Form of a Law from that which is commanded to be done to one single Person, first you are not ignorant (for Logick hath taught you that) what a great absurdity you will make, next you will be in danger to be assaulted by the opposers of Tyranny with the like weapons; for you must either shew what singular thing there is in that matter, or propose it to be imitated by all every where, or if you cannot do this, you must acknowledge, that whatever is enjoyned concerning any one Person by any special command of God, it doth alike belong to all. If you shall once admit this (which you must needs do) it will be instantly objected, that *Ahab* was killed by Gods command, and a reward was also promised and performed to him that should kill him. Whenever therefore you betake your self to that refuge, you must obey all Tyrants: because God by his Prophet did command his People to obey one Tyrant. It will be instantly replyed, that all Tyrants ought also to be killed, because *Ahab* at the command of God was killed by the Captain of his host. Therefore I advise you to provide a more firm defence from Scripture for Tyrants, or then laying the same a side at present you may have your recourse to the Philosophers, phets School. *M.* I shall indeed think upon it. But in the mean time let us return from whence we have digressed. What do you bring from Scripture, why Tyrants may be lawfully killed. *B.* First of all I proffer this, that seing it is expresly commanded to cut off wickedness and wicked Men, without any exception of rank or degree, and yet in no place of sacred Scripture are Tyrants more spared than private Persons. Next, that the definition of Powers delivered by *Paul* doth not wholly belong to Tyrants, because they accommodate not the strength of their Authority, for the benefit of the People, but for fulfilling their own Lusts. Further we should diligently consider how much Power *Paul* doth grant to Bishops, whose Function he doth highly and truly praise, as being some way like unto Kings, as far as the nature of both their Functions can admit. For Bishops are Physitians of Internal Diseases, as Kings are Physitians of external Distempers, and yet he would neither of them to be free from or not liable to the Jurisdiction of the other. And even as Bishops are subject to Kings in the Exercise of their Civil Government, so ought Kings obey the Spiritual admonitions of Bishops. Now albeit the amplitude and dignity of Bishops be so great, yet no Law divine nor humane doth exempt them from the punishment of crimes. And to pass by others. The very Pope who is accounted the Bishop of Bishops, who so exalts himself above all Kings, that he should be accounted a certain God amongst them, yet is he not exempted from the Punishment of Laws, no not by his own Canonists, a kind of men very devoted to him. For seing they would think it absurd that God (for they do not hesitate to call him thus) should be obnoxious to Mens censure, and think it unjust that the greatest crimes and most filthy abominations should pass unpunished in any, and yet they have found out a way whereby crimes may be punished, and the Pope accounted sacred and inviolable. For the Priviledge of the Pope is one thing, and of that Man who is Pope is another, say they and whilst they exempt the Pope (whom they deny can err) from the cognition of the Laws, yet do they confess him to be a Man obnoxious to vices and punishment of vices ; nor have the more subtilly than severely declared their Judgment herein. It would be tedious to rehearse, what Popes (to speak after their usual way) what Men personating Popes, who not only alive were forced to renounce their Popedom, but being dead were pulled out of their Graves, and thrown into *Tiber*. But to omit old Histories. The recent memory of Pope *Paul* the *IV.* is fresh in our mind, for his own *Rome* did witness

ness a publick hatred against him by a new kind of Decree. For they vented their Fury (he being by death taken away) against his nearest Kinsfolk, his Statues and painted Images or Pictures. Nor should this Interpretation seem more subtile, whereby we separate the Power, from the Person in Power, than Philosophy doth acknowledge, and the antient Interpreters do approve, nor is the rude multitude and Strangers to subtile disputing ignorant thereof; for the meerest Tradesmen take it for no blot upon their Trade, if a Smith or Baker be hanged for robbery, but are rather glad that their society is purged of such Villains. But if there be any of another mind, I think it is to be feared, that he seems to be rather grieved at those Mens Punishment with whom he is associate in their Villany, than for the Infamy of their Society. I am of the opinion, if Kings would abandon the Councils of wicked Men and Flatterers, and measure their own Greatness rather by duties of vertue, than by the impunity of evil deeds, they would not be grieved for the Punishment of Tyrants, nor think that Royal Majesty is lessened by whatsoever destruction of Tyrants, but rather be glad that it is purged from a most filthy blot of wickedness; especially seeing they use to be highly offended with robbers, and that very justly, if any of them in their malefices pretend the Kings Name. *M.* Forsooth, they have just Cause. But laying these things aside, I would have you go on to the other head you proposed. *B.* What heads do you mean? *M.* Namely in what time, and to whom *Paul* wrote those things, for I desire to know what the knowledg thereof doth make for the argument in hand. *B.* I shall herein obey you also. And first I shall speak of the time, *Paul* wrote these things in the very Infancy of the Church, in which time it was not only necessary to be blameless, but none was to give occasion to such as sought occasion of reproaching, and unjust causes of staining the Professors of Christianity: Next he wrote to Men of several Nations, and so gathered together into one society out of the whole body of the *Roman* Empire, amongst whom there were but few very rich, yea almost none, who either had ruled, or could rule, or were in any great account amongst their fellow Citizens, they were not so many in number, and these almost but strangers, and for the most part but lately freed of bondage, and others but Tradesmen and Servants. Amongst them there were many who did further pretend Christian Liberty, than the simplicity of the Gospel could suffer. Now this company of People out of the promiscuous Multitude; which did won their Living, though meanly, by hard labour, was not to be so careful of the state of the Commonwealth

wealth, of the Majesty of the Empire, and of the conversation and duty of Kings, as of the publick tranquility, and their domestick Affairs, nor could they justly claim any more, than to lye lurking under the shadow of whatever Government they were under. If that People had attempted to lay hold upon any Part of Government they should have been accounted not only foolish, but mad. Nor should they come out of their lurking holes to breed trouble to those that did hold the helm of publick affairs in hand. Immature Licentiousness was also to be repressed, an unfit Interpreter of Christian Liberty. What then doth *Paul* write? doubtless no new precept but only these usual precepts, namely, that Subjects should obey their Rulers, Servants their Masters and Wives their Husbands, nor should we think the Lords yoke, how light soever, doth liberate us of the bonds of our duty, but with a more attentive mind than before to be bound thereunto, so that we should omit nothing through all the degrees of duties in our relations, that might any wise make for acquiring the favour and good Will of Men. And so it should come to pass, that the Name of God should be well spoken of among the *Gentiles* because of us, and the Glory of the Gospel more largely propagated. For performing of these things, there was need of publick Peace, the keepers whereof were Princes and Magistrates, albeit wicked. May it please you, that I set before you a manifest representation hereof? Imagin that one of our Doctors doth write to the Christians, that live under the *Turks*, to men, I say, of mean Fortune, sore dejected in mind, weak and few in Number, and exposed to the injuries of all and every one. What else, I ask you, would he advise them, then what *Paul* did advise the Church that then was at *Rome*, or what *Jeremy* advised the exiles in *Assyria*? Now this is a most sure argument that *Paul* had a regard to those mens condition to whom he did write, and not to all others, because he diligently sets home the mutual duties of Husbands toward their Wives, of Wives towards their Husbands, of Parents towards their Children, and of Children towards their Parents, of Servants towards their Masters and of Masters towards their Servants. And albeit he writes what the duty of Magistrates is, yet he doth not give them any particular compellation, (as he had done in the preceeding relations.) For which cause we shall judge that he gave no other precepts for Kings and others in Authority: especially seeing their lust was to be much more restrained, than that of private persons? What other cause may we imagin, than that at that time there were no Kings or Magistrates in the Church to whom
he

he might write? Imagin that *Paul* doth now live in our days, wherein not only the People, but Princes also Profess Christianity. At the same time, let there be some Prince, who doth conceive that not only should human Laws but also divine Laws be subject to his lust and pleasure, and who will have not only his decrees, but also his very nods to be accounted for Laws, like that man in the Gospel, who neither did fear God, nor reverence man, who distributs the Church revenues amongst villains and rascals, if I may so say; and doth mock the sincere Worshipers of God, and accounts them but Fools and mad Men, or Fanaticks: what would *Paul* write of such to the Church? If he were like himself, he would certainly deny that he should be accounted a Magistrate. He would interdict all Christians to have any communion with him, either in dyet, Speech, or converse, and leave him to the People to be punished by the Laws, and would think they did nothing but their duty, if they should account him not to be their King, with whom they were to have no Fellowship by the Law of God. But there will not be wanting some Court-slaves, or Sycophants, who, finding no honest refuge, become so impudent, as to say, that God being angry against a people doth set *Tyrants* over them: whom as hangmen he appoints for punishing them. Which to be true I do confess; yet it is as true, that God many times doth stir up from amongst the lowest of the people some very mean, and obscure men to revenge Tyranical Pride and weakness: For God, (as before is said) doth command wicked men to be cut off: and doth except neither degree, sex, or condition, nor yet any man. For Kings are not more acceptable to him than beggars. Therefore, we may truely aver, that God being alike the Father of all, to whose providence nothing lies hid, and whose power nothing can resist, will not leave any wickedness unpunished. Moreover, another will stand up and ask some example out of Scripture of a King punished by his Subjects: which albeit I could not produce, yet it will not presently follow, that because we do not read such a thing therein to have been done, that it should be accounted for an high crime and malifice. I may rehearse among many Nations very many and sound Laws, whereof in holy write there is no example. For as the consent of all Nations doth approve, that what the Law doth command, is accounted just, and what it forbiddeth, is unjust, so since the memory of man it was never forbidden, that what should not be contained in Laws, should not at all be done. For that servitude was never received,

nor

The due Priviledge of the Scotch *Government.*

nor will the Nature of things so fruitful of new Examples suffer the same to be received, that whatever is not by some Law commanded, or recorded by some famous Example, should be accounted for a great Crime and Malifice. If therefore any man shall ask of me an Example out of the Sacred Scriptures, wherein the Punishment of wicked Kings is approved, I shall again ask him, where is the same reprehended? But if nothing done without some Example doth please: how many civil Statutes shall we have continued with us? how many Laws, for the greatest part thereof is not taken out of any old Example, but established against new Deceits, and that without Example. But we have already answered those that require Examples more than was needful: Now if the Jewish Kings were not punished by their Subjects, they make not much for our purpose in hand. For they were not at first created by the People, but were by God given them. And therefore very justly, he who was the Author of that Honour, was to punish their Misdeeds. But we debate, that the People, from whom our Kings enjoy whatever Priviledge they claim, is more powerful than their Kings; and that the whole People have that same Priviledge over them, which they have over every one in particular of the whole People. All the Rights and Priviledges of forraign Nations, who live under lawful Kings, do make for us; all the Nations which are subject to Kings chosen by themselves, do commonly agree herein, that whatever Priviledge the People hath given to any, the same they may require again very justly. All Common-wealths have still retained this Priviledge. Therefore *Lentulus,* having conspired with *Cataline* for overturning the Common wealth of *Rome,* was compelled to renounce his Prætorship, and the *Decemviri,* the Makers of the *Roman* Laws, were taken orders with, even whilst they enjoyed the Supream Authority; Some Dukes of *Venice,* and *Chilpericus* King of *France,* laying aside their Royal Honours, as private Men, spent their Days in Monasteries. And not long ago, *Christiernus* King of the *Danes,* twenty years almost after he was deprived of his Kingdom, did end his Life in Prison. Now the Dictatorship (which was a Kind of Tyranny) was in the Peoples Power. And this Privilege hath been constantly observed, that publick Benefices granted amiss, and the Liberty granted to ingrate Persons set at liberty (whom Laws do very much favour) might be taken back again. These things we have spoken of forraign Nations, lest we alone seem to have usurped any new Priviledge, against our Kings. But as to what doth properly belong to us, the matter might have been handled in few Words. *M.* What way? For this I am very desirous to hear. *B.* I might enumerate twelve or more Kings, who for great Crimes and flagitious deeds, have been either adjudged to perpetual Imprisonment, or escaped the just Punishment of their Wickedness, either by Exile or voluntary Death. But left any blame me for relating old and obsolete Stories, if I should make mention of *Culen*, *Evan* and *Ferchard*, I shall produce some few within the Memory of our Fore-fathers. All the Estates in a publick Convention, judged *James* the Third to have been justly killed, for his great Cruelty and flagitious Wickedness towards his Subjects, and did caution that none of them who had aided, consented, or contributed Money, or had been active therein, to be called thereafter into question therefore. That they therefore did judge the Deed to be duly and orderly done, it being once down, doubtless they desired it might be set down for an Example in time coming, surely no less than *L. Quintius*, sitting in Judgment, did commend *Servilius Ahalus* for having killed before the Bench, *Sp. Mellus* turning his Back, and refusing to compear into Judgment, and that he was not guilty of Blood-shed, but thought him to be Nobilitate by the Slaughter of a *Tyrant*, and all Posterity did affirm the same. What Subject hath ever approved the Slaughter of one affecting Tyranny? What do you suppose would he have done with a *Tyrant* robbing the Goods of his Subjects, and shedding their Blood? What hath our Men done? do not they seem to have made a Law, who by a publick Decree, without any Punishment, have past by a flagitious Crime committed, if such like shall happen in time coming? for at most there is no difference, whether you judge concerning that which is done, or make a Law concerning what is to be done. For both ways a Judgment is past concerning the Kind of the Crime, and concerning the Punishment or Reward of the Actor. *M.* These things will perhaps have some weight amongst us. But I know not how other Nations abroad will take them. You see I must satisfie them. Not as in a judicial way I were to be called in question for the Crime, but openly amongst all concerning the Fame, not mine (for I am far from any Suspition thereof) but of my Country men. For I am afraid, lest forraign Nations will rather blame the Decrees, wherewith you suppose you are sufficiently protected, than the Crime it self full of Cruelty and Hatred. But you know, if I mistake not, what is usually spoken according to the Disposition and Opinion of every one on both hands, concerning the Examples you have proposed. I would therefore (because you seem to have expected what is past, not so much from the Decrees of Men, as from the Springs of Nature) you would briefly expound, if you have ought to say for the Equity of that Law. *B.* Albeit that

may

The due Priviledge of the Scotch Government. 57

may seem unjust to stand at the Bar to plead amongst Forreigners for a Law approved from the very first Times of our *Scots* Government by Kings, by the constant Practice of so many Ages ago, necessary for the People, not unjust for Kings, but lawful, but now at last accused of Illegality; yet for your Sake I shall try it. And as if I were debating with those very Men who would trouble you, I first ask this. What do you think here worthy of Reprehension? Is it the Cause? why is it sought for? or is it the Law it self which you reprehended? for the Law was sought for repressing the unjust Lusts of Kings. Whoever doth condemn this, must likewise condemn all the Laws of all Nations, for all Laws were desired for the very same Cause. Do you reprehend the Law it self? do you think it lawful that Kings be exempted of, or not liable to the Laws? let us then see if that be also expedient. And for proving that it is not expedient for the People, there needs not many Words. For if in the former Discourse we have rightly compared a King to a Physitian, as it is not expedient for People that Impunity be permitted to a Physitian for killing whom he pleaseth, so it is not for the Good of all, that a promiscuous Licence be granted to Kingss for making Havock of all. We have no cause then to be offended with a People, whose chief Power it is in making Laws, if, as they desire a good King to be set over them, even so a Law to be set over a King none of the best. But if this Law be not for the Kings Use or Profit, let us see if the People should be dealt with to remit somewhat of their Priviledge, and of abrogating it not for the space of three days, but according to our usual way we indict a Parliament to meet within forty days. In the mean time, that we may reason together concerning the Law, tell me, doth he seem to respect the Good of a mad Man, who looseth his Bonds? *M.* Not at all. *B.* What do you think of him who giveth to a Man sick of a Fever, so as he is not far from Madness, a Drink of cold Water, though earnestly craving it, do you think he deserveth well of that sick Man? *M.* But I speak of Kings of a sound Mind. I deny that there is any need of Medicine for such as are in Health, nor of Laws for Kings of a sound Mind. But you would have all Kings to seem wicked, for you impose Laws upon all. *B.* I do not think that all Kings are Wicked. Nor do I think all the People to be wicked, and yet the Law in one Voice doth speak to the whole People. Now wicked Men are afraid at that Voice, good People do not think it belongs to them. Thus good Kings have no cause to be offended at this Law, and wicked Kings, if they were wise, would render Thanks to the Law-giver, who hath ordained what he understood would not be

profita-

profitable for them, nor to be lawful for them to do. Which indeed they will not do, if so be they shall once return again to their right Mind. Even as they who are restored to Health do render Thanks to their Physitian, whom before they had hated, because he would not grant their Desires whilst they were sick. But if Kings continue in their Madness, whoever doth most obey them, is to be judged their greatest Enemy. Of this sort are Flatterers, who by flattering their Vices, do cherish and increase their Disease, and at last, together almost with Kings, are utterly ruined. *M.* I cannot indeed deny, but that such Princes have been, and may be restrained by Law-bonds. For there is no Monster more violent and more pestiferous than Man, when (as it is in the Poets Fables) he is once degenerated into a Beast. *B.* You would much more say so, if you consider how many ways a Man becomes a Beast, and of how many several Monsters he is made. Which thing the old Poets did acutely observe and notably express, when they say that *Prometheus*, in the framing of Man, did give him some Particle out of every living Creature. It would be an infinite Work for me to relate the Natures of all one by one. But certainly two most vile Monsters do evidently appear in Man, Wrath and Lust. But what else do Laws act or desire, but that these Monsters be obedient to right Reason? and whilst they do not obey Reason, may not Laws, by the Bonds of their Sanctions restrain them? whoever then doth loose a King, or any other from these Bonds, doth not loose one Man, but throws in against Reason two Monsters exceeding cruel, and armeth them for breaking asunder the Bars of Laws: so that *Aristotle* seemeth to have rightly and truly said, that he who obeyeth the Law, doth obey both God and the Law; but he that obeyeth the King, doth obey both a Man and a Beast. *M.* Albeit these things seem to be said appositely enough, yet I think we are in a Mistake two ways. First, because the last things we have spoken, seem not to agree well enough with the first. Next, because, as we may well know we seem not to have yet come to the main Point of our Debate. For a little before we were at agreement that the Voice of the King and Law ought to be the same, here again we make him Subject to the Laws. Now though we grant this to be very true, what have we gained by this Conclusion? for who shall call to an account a King become a Tyrant? for I fear a Priviledge without Strength will not be powerful enough to restrain a King forgetful of his Duty, and unwilling to be drawn unto Judgment, to answer for Maleadministration. *B.* I fear ye have not well pondered what we have before debated, concerning the Royal Power. For if ye had well considered

dered it, you had eafily underftood what you now have faid, that betwixt them there is no Contradiction. But that you may the more eafily take it up, firft anfwer we, when a Magiftrate or Clerk doth utter the Words of a Proclamation before an *Herauld*. Is not the Voice of both one and the fame? I fay of an Herauld, and of a Clerk. *M.* It is the fame indeed. *B.* Which of the two feems greateft? *M.* He who firft doth utter the Words. What is the King, who is the Author of the Edict? *M.* Greater than both. *B.* Then according to this Similitude let us fet down the King, the Law, and the People. The Voice is the fame both of King and Law. Which of the two hath the Authority from the other, the King from the Law, or the Law from the King? *M.* The King from the Law. *B.* From whence collect you that? *M.* Becaufe the King was not fought for to reftrain the Law, but the Law to reftrain the King. And from the Law he hath that, whereby he is a King, for without the Law he would be a Tyrant. *B.* The Law then is more powerful than the King, and is as a Governefs and Moderatrix both of his Luft and Actions. *M.* That is already granted. *B.* What, Is not the Voice of the People and the Law the fame? *M.* The very fame. *B.* Which of the two is moft powerful, the People or the Law? *M.* I think, the whole People. *B.* Why do you think fo? *M.* Becaufe the People is as it were the Parent of the Law, certainly the Author thereof, they being able to make or abrogate it as they pleafe. *B.* Seeing then the Law is more powerful than the King, and the People more powerful than the Law, we muft fee before which we may call the King to anfwer in Judgment. Let us alfo difcufs this. Are not the things which for fome others Sake are inftituted, of lefs account than thofe for whofe fake they are required or fought? *M.* I would have that more clearly explained. *B.* Follow me thus, is not a Bridle made for the Horfe Sake? *M.* It is fo. *B.* Are not Saddles, Girdings and Spurs made for Horfes? *M.* They are. *B.* Now if there were no Horfe, there fhould be no ufe of fuch things. *M.* None at all. *B.* A Horfe is then better than all thefe. *M.* Why not? *B.* Why a Horfe? for what ufe is he defired? *M.* For very many Ufes, and firft of all, for obtaining Victory in War. *B.* We therefore do efteem the Victory to be of more worth than Horfes, Arms, and other things, which are prepared for the Ufe of War. *M.* Of more worth indeed it is. *B.* What did men efpecially regard in creating a King? *M.* The Peoples Good, as I fuppofe. *B.* But would there be no need of Kings, if there were no Societies of Men? *M.* None at all. *B.* The People then is better than the King. *M.* It muft needs be fo. *B.* If the People be better, they are alfo
greater.

greater. *M.* But when shall we hope for that Happiness, that the whole People agree unto that which is Right. *B.* That indeed is scarce to be hoped for. And to expect it, is certainly needless: otherwise a Law could neither be made, nor a Magistrate Created. For neither is almost any Law alike to all, nor is there almost any Man in that Popular Favour, so as to have no Man either an Enemy to him, or Envious or Slanderer of him; this now is desired, that the Law be useful for the greatest part, and that the greatest part have a good opinion of him that is to be chosen. What if the greatest part of the People may enjoyn a Law to be made, and Create a Magistrate, what doth hinder, but that they also may judge him, and appoint Judges over him? Or if the *Tribunes* of the People of *Rome*, and the *Lacedemonian Ephori* were sought to modifie the Power of Magistracy, should it seem unjust to any Man, if a Free-People, either upon the like or different account, did foresee their own good in suppressing the bitterness of Tyranny? *M.* Now I seem almost to perceive what a People can do: But it is a matter of difficulty to judge what they will do, or appoint to be done. For the greatest part almost doth require Old and usual Customes, and hateth Novelty, which the rather is to be admired, seeing there is so great an inconstancy in Meat, Apparel, Buildings, and in all Houshold Furniture. *B.* Do not think that these things are spoken by me, that I would have any new thing in this kind to be done, but that I might shew you it hath been of Old, that a King should answer in judgment before Judges, which you did believe to be almost Incredible, or at least a Novelty. For to pass over, how often it hath been done by our Ancestors, as partly before we have said, and you may also easily Collect from History; did you never hear of those who contended for the Kingdom to have appealed to Arbiters? *M.* I have indeed heard it to have been sometimes done amongst the *Persians*. *B.* And our Writers affirm that the same was done by *Grimas* and *Milcolumbus*. But least you alledg that that kind of Arbiters were wont to be assumed by the Contenders own consent, let us come to the ordinary Judges. *M.* Here I am afraid you may as far prevail, as if a Man should spread Nets in the Sea to catch *Whales*. *B.* Why so, I pray you? *M.* Because all apprehending, restraint and punishment is carried on by the more powerful against the weaker. But before what Judges will you command a King to compear? Before them over whom he hath the Supream Power to judge? Whom he can compesce by this one word, *I Forbid*? *B.* What if some greater Power be found which hath that right priviledge or jurisdiction over Kings, which Kings have over others? *M.* I desire to hear that. *B.* We told you, if you remember,

The due Priviledge of the Scotch *Government.*

member, that this Power is in the People. *M.* In the whole People indeed, or in the greatest part thereof. I also yield thus further, that it is in those to whom the People, or the greatest part of them shall transmit that Power. *B.* You do well, in holding in my pains. *M.* But you know that the greatest part of the People is corrupted either through fear, or reward, or through some hope of a Bribe and Impunity, so as they prefer their own benefit and pleasures or lusts to the publick utility, and also safety. Now there are very few who are not hereby moved: according to that of the Poet. Good People are indeed Rare, scarce so many in number, as there be Gates in *Thebes,* or Issues of the *River Nilus.* Now all the rest being a naughty Rabble fatned with Blood and rapine enjoy their Venal liberty, and Envy the liberty of others. Now that I may pass from those with whom the name of wicked Kings also is sacred. I also Omit those, who, albeit they are not ignorant what is lawful and just or right, yet prefer a quiet sloathfulness to honest hazards, and hesitating in their minds do frame their consultation on the expectation of the Event: or follow the good Fortune of either party, but not the cause. How great this multitude will be, you see. *B.* Great indeed: but yet not very great. For the wrong of Tyrants may reach many, but their good Deeds very few. For the Avarice of the vulgar is insatiable, as a fire is the more vehemently kindled by adding Fuel thereto: But what is by force taken away from many, doth rather increase the Hunger of some few, then Satiate their Lust. And further the fidelity of such Men for the most part is unstable: As saith the Poet. Fidelity doth stand and fall with Fortune. But if they would also continue firm in their judgment, they should not be accounted in the number of good Subjects, for they are the Violators, or rather Betrayers of humane Society; which Vice if not sufferable in a King, is far less tolerable in a private Person. Who then are to be accounted the right Subjects? They who give Obedience to the Laws, maintain and defend humane Society, who rather undergo all pains and Labours, and all Hazards for common Safety, then spend their time Sluggishly in Idleness void of all Honesty; who set before their Eyes, not their present enjoyments, but the remembrance of Eternity. But if there be any whom fear and self interest recal from Hazards, yet the splendor of some notable Atchievment, and the Beauty of Vertue will raise up dejected minds; and those who dare not be Authors or Leaders, will not decline to become Associates. If therefore Subjects be reckoned, not by number, but by dignity and worth, not only the better part, but also the greater part will stand for their liberty, honesty and safety. But if the whole com-

mon

mon People diffent, this fays nothing to our prefent debate: For we demand not what is to be done, but what may lawfully be done. But now let us come to the ordinary judicial Sentences. *M.* That I juſt now look for. *B.* If any private Man contend that his inheritance, or fome part of his Land is unjuſtly detained by the King, what do you think fhould this private Man do? Shall he paſs from his Land, becauſe he cannot fet a Judge over the King? *M.* Not at all, but he may command not the King, but his proxy to compear in judgment. *B.* Now fee what ſtrength that refuge hath whereof you make uſe. For it is all one to me, whether the King compear, or his Proxy, or Advocate, for both ways, the Litif-conteſtation will redound to the Kings loſs: The damage or gain will redound to him not to his Advocate by the Event of the Sentence. In the end he is found Guilty, that is, he whoſe cauſe is agitated. Now I would have you confider not only how abfurd it is, but alſo unjuſt to paſs Sentence againſt a King for a petty inheritance for Lights in a Houfe, or for eafe droppings thereof, and no Sentence to be paſt for Paricide, Witch-craft or Treafon. To make uſe of the feverity of the Law in leſſer matters, and the greateſt Licenſe and Impunity to be permitted in the greateſt Crimes. So that that Old Proverb feems plainly true, Laws are very like Spiders Webs, which hold flies faſt, but let bigger Beaſts paſt through. Nor is that complaint and indignation of fome juſt, who fay that it is neither Honeſt nor Equitable, that judgment fhould paſs againſt a King, by a Man of an inferiour Rank, feeing they fee it received and admitted in debate about Mony or Land; and the greateſt Peers next to the King for the moſt part compear before the Judges, who are inferior to them in riches, nobility, and valour. And not much above the Vulgar Rank: and far more below the guilty, than the greateſt Peers are below Kings. Nor yet for all this do thefe Noble-Men or Peers think it any Derogation to their Dignity. Now if we ſhall once admit this, that no Man can be lifted before a Judge, unleſs the Judge be every way Superiour to the Perfon Arraigned, the Inferiour Rank muſt attend and wait on until the King either pleafe, or be at leifure, to cognofce concerning the guilty Noble-Man, but what if their complaint be not only unjuſt, but alſo falfe? For no Man coming before a Judge doth come before an Inferior Perſon, efpecially feeing fo great an Honour is by God himfelf conferred upon the Order of Judges, that he calleth them not only Kings but alſo Gods, and as much as can be, doth Communicate to them his own Dignity. Therefore thofe *Roman Popes,* who did gracioufly Indulge Kings to Kiſs their Feet, who did fend for Honours like to fuch as came to meet them, their *Mules* who did Tread
upon

upon the Necks of *Emperours*, being called to answer in judgment, did obey, and being compelled by Judges, renounced their *Popedm*. *John* the Twenty Second being from flight brought back, was thrust into Prison, and scarce at last relieved by Mony, and submitted to him that was put into his place, and therefore he did approve the Sentence of the Judges. What did the *Synode* of *Basil*? Did it not appoint and ordain by the common consent of all the Members thereof, that the *Pope* is subject to the Council of Priests. Now these Fathers were perswaded upon what account they did so, which you may find out of the Acts of these Councils. Kings then who confess the Majesty of *Popes* to be so far above them, as that it doth over-shadow them all with the Top of its Celsitude, I know not how they think therein their Dignity to be diminished, wherein the *Pope* did not think he was disparaged to descend from so High a Throne, namely, to stand to the Judgment and Sentence of the Cardinals: Hereby you may see how false their complaint is, who disdain to be Arraigned at the Bar of an Inferior Judge, for it is not *Titius Sempronius*, or *Stichus* that doth in a judiciary way Condemn and Assoil, but the Law, to which Kings should yield Obedience. The most famous Emperours *Theodosius* and *Valentinianus* accounted honourable. I shall here set down their own words, because they deserve the Memory of all Ages. Is is (say they) a word well beseeming the Majesty of a King to confess he is a Prince tied to the Laws. And we declare that it is more to submit a principality to the Laws than to enjoy an Empire. And what we now declare by this our Edict, we will not suffer to be infringed. These things the very best Princes judged right and by Law Established, and some of the worst see the same. For *Nero* being Apparelled in a dress of Harpers, is said to have not only observed their Carriage and Motions, but also when it came to be judged who had done best, that he stood Solicitous betwixt Hope and Fear for the Victory. For albeit he knew he would be declared Victor, yet he thought the Victory would be the more Honest, if he should obtain it, not by the Flattery of the Judges, but by due debate: And he thought the Observation of the Law did Contribute not for the Diminuition of his Authority, but for the splendor of the Victory. *M.* Your discourse, I perceive, is not so Insolent, as at first I took it, when you said, you would have Kings Obedient to the Laws: For it is not so much founded upon the Aurhority of *Phylosophers*, as of *Kings*, *Emperours* and *Councils* of the Church. *M.* But I do not well understand that you say, it is not Man but the Law that Judgeth. *B.* Call to mind what was said a little before: Did we not say, that the Voice of the King and of the Law is the same? *M.* We did fo. B. What the Voice of the Clerk, and *Herauld* is, when the Law is publifhed? M. The very fame. B. But which of the two hath the Authority from the other, whether the Judge from the Law, or the Law from the Judge? M. The Judge from the Law. B. The ftrength of the Sentence is then from the Law, and the pronounciation of the words of the Law alone is the Judges. M. It feems fo. B. Yea, there is nothing more certain, for the Sentences of Judges pronounced according to the Law are ratified, elfe they are refcinded. M. There is nothing more true than that. B. You fee then that the Judges Authority is from the Law, and not the Laws Authority from the Judge. M. I fee it is fo. B. The low and mean condition of him that Proclaimeth the Law doth not diminifh the Dignity thereof, but the Dignity of the Laws is ftill the fame, whether the King, a Judge, or an *Herauld* Proclaim it. M. It is fo indeed. B. The Law then being once Eftablifhed, is firft the Voice of the King, and then of others. M. It is fo. B. Whilft then the King is condemned by a Judge, he feems to be condemned by the Law. M. That is very clear. B. If by the Law, then he is condemned by his own Voice, as feems, no lefs than, if it were written with his own hand. B. Why then do we fo much weary our felves concerning a Judge, feeing we have the Kings own Confeffion, that is to fay, the Law? Let us alfo confider this, which is but prefently come into my mind. When a King in what Caufe foever doth fit in judgment as a Judge, fhould he not lay a fide the perfon of all others, and to have no refpect to Brother, Kifman, Friend or Foe, but retain only the perfon of a Judge. M. He ought fo to do. B. Ought he not to remember that Perfon only, whofe proper Act it is he is about. M. I would have you tell me that more clearly. B. Take heed then: when any Man doth fecretly take away another Mans Goods, what do we fay he hath done? M. I think, he hath ftollen them. B. How do you call him for this deed? M. A Thief. B. How do you fay he hath done, who makes ufe of his Neighbours Wife, as his own? M. We fay he hath committed Adultery. B. How do we call him? M. An Adulterer. B. How do we call him that judgeth? M. A Judge. B. To others alfo after this manner from the Actions they are about, names may be rightly given. M. They may. B. When a King then is to pafs a Sentence, he is to lay afide all other Perfons. M. Indeed he fhould, efpecially thofe that may prejudge either of the Parties in Judging. B. How do you call him againft whom the Sentence is paft, from that Act of judgment? M. We may call him Guilty. B. And is it not equitable that a Judge lay afide fuch perfons as may prejudge the Sentence? M. Certainly he fhould, if fo be, fuch perfons be more regarded than the

caufe:

The due Priviledge of the Scotch *Government.* 65

cause : Yet such persons pertain not to a Judge. Seeing God will have no respect to be had to the poor in judgment. *B.* If then any Man, who is a Painter and a Grammarian debate before a Judge concerning the Art of Painting against a Painter, he is not a Grammarian, for the Science of Grammar should not herein avail him. *M.* Nothing at all. *B.* Nor the Art of Painting avail the other, if the debate be concerning Grammar. *M.* Not a whit more. *B.* A Judge then in judgment must acknowledge but one name, to wit, of the Crime, or guilt, whereof the Adversary or Plantiff doth accuse his Party or Defendant to be guilty. *M.* No more. *B.* What if a King be guilty of Parricide, hath he the name of a King, and whatever doth belong to a Judge? *M.* Nothing at all, but only of a Parricide, for he cometh not into Controversie concerning his Kingdom, but concerning his Parricide. *B.* What if two Parricides be called to answer in judgment, the one a King, and the other a Poor Fellow, shall not there be alike way of procedure by the Judge of both ? *M.* The very same with both, so that I think that of *Lucan* is no less true than Elegantly spoken. *viz.* *Cæsar* was both my Leader and Fellow in passing over the *Rhine.* Whom a Malifice doth make guilty, it maketh alike. *B.* True indeed. The process then is not here carried on against a King and a Poor Man, but against their Parricides: For then the process should be led on concerning the King, if it should be asked which of the two ought to be King ; Or if it come into question, whether *Hiero* be King or a *Tyrant,* or if any other thing come into question which doth properly belong to the Kings Function. Even as if the Sentence be concerning a Painter, when it is demanded, hath he skill in the Art of Painting. *M.* What if a King will not willingly compear, nor by force can be compelled to compear. *B.* Then the case is common with him as with all other Flagitious persons. For no Thief or Warlike will willingly compear before a Judge to be judged. But I suppose, you know, what the Law doth permit, namely to kill any way a Thief Stealing by Night, and also to kill him if he defend himself when Stealing by day. But if he cannot be drawn to compear to answer but by Force, you remember what is usually done. For we persue by Force and Arms such Robbers as are more powerful than that by Law they can be reached. Nor is there almost any other cause of all the Wars betwixt Nations, People and Kings than those injuries, which, whilst they cannot be determined by Justice, are by Arms decided. *M.* Against Enemies indeed for these Causes Wars use to be carried on, but the case is far otherwise with Kings, to whom by a most sacred Oath interposed we are bound to give Obedience. *B.* We are indeed bound : But they do first promise that they shall Rule in Equity and Justice. *M.* It is so. *B.* There is then a mutual

tual paction betwixt the King and his Subjects. *M.* It seems so. *B.* doth not he who first recedes from what is covenanted, and doth contrary to what he hath covenanted to do, break the Contract and Covenant? *M.* He doth *B.* The Bond then being loosed, which did hold fast the King with the People, whatever priviledg or right did belong to him, by that agreement and covenant who looseth the same, I suppose is lost. *M.* It is lost. *B.* He then with whom the Covenant was made becometh as free as ever it was before the stipulation. *M.* He doth clearly enjoy the same priviledge, and the same liberty. *B.* Now if a King do those things which are directly for the dissolution of Society, for the continuance whereof he was created, how do we call him? *M.* A Tyrant, I suppose. *B.* now a *Tyrant* hath not only no just authority over a People, but is also their Enemy, *M.* He is indeed an Enemy. *B.* Is there not a just and lawful War with an Enemy for grievous and intolerable injuries? *M.* It is forsooth a just War. *B.* what War is that which is carried on with him who is the Enemy of all Mankind, that is, a *Tyrant*? *M.* A most just War. *B.* Now a lawful War being once under taken with an Enemy, and for a just cause, it is lawful not only for the whole People to kill that Enemy, but for every one of them. *M.* I confess that. *B.* May not every one out of the whole multitude of Mankind assault with all the Calamities of War, a *Tyrant* who is a publick Enemy, with whom all good Men have a perpetual warfare. *M.* I perceive all Nations almost to have been of that Opinion. For *Thebe* is usually commended for killing her Husband, *Timoleon* for killing his Brother, and *Cassius* for killing his Son: and *Fulvius* for killing his own Son going to *Catiline*, and *Brutus* for killing his own Sons and Kinsmen; having understood they had conspired to introduce Tyranny again: and publick rewards were appointed to be given, and honours appointed by several Cities of *Greece* to those that should kill *Tyrants*. So that (as is before said) they thought there was no Bond of humanity to be kept with Tyrants. But why do I collect the assent of some single Persons, since I can produce the testimony almost of the whole World. For who doth not sharply rebuke *Domitius Corbulo* for neglecting the safety of Mankind, who did not thrust *Nero* out of his Empire, when he might very easily have done it? And not only was he by the *Romans* reprehended, but by *Tyridates* the *Persian* King, being not afraid; lest at all it should afterward befal an Example unto himself. But the Minds of most wicked Men enraged with cruelty, are not so void of this publick hatred against Tyrants, but that sometimes it breaketh out in them against their will, and forceth them to stand amazed with terrour at the light of such a just and lawful deed. When the Ministers of *Cajus Caligula* a most cruel Tyrant

were

were with the like cruelty tumultuating, for the slaughter of their Lord and Master, and required those that had killed him to be punished, now and then crying aloud, who had killed the Emperour: *Valerius Asiaticus* one of the Senators standing in an eminent high place from whence he might be heard, cryed out aloud: I wish I had killed him. At which word these tumultuary Persons void of all humanity stood as it were astonished, and so forbore any more to cry out tumultuously. For there is so great force in an honest deed, that the very lightest shew thereof, being presented to the Minds of Men, the most violent assaults are allayed, and fierce fury doth languish, and madness nill it will it doth acknowledge the soveraignty of reason. Neither are they of another judgment, who with their loud crys mix Heaven and Earth together. Now this we do easily understand either from hence, that they do reprehend what now is done, but do commend and approve the same seemingly more atrocious, when they are recorded in an old History: and thereby do evidently demonstrate that they are more obsequious to their own particular affections, than moved by any publick dammage. But why do we seek a more certain witness what Tyrants do deserve, than their own Conscience? thence is that perpetual fear from all, and chiefly from good Men; and they do constantly see hanging above their own Necks, the Sword which they hold still drawn against others, and by their own hatred against others the measure other Mens Minds against them. But contrariwise good Men, by fearing no Man do often procure their own hazard, whilst they weigh the good will of others towards them, not from the vicious nature of Men, but from their own desert towards others. *B.* You do then judge that to be true, that Tyrants are to be reckoned in the number of the most cruel Brute Beasts; and that Tyranical violence is more unatural than Poverty, Sickness, Death, and other miseries which may befall Men naturally. *M.* Indeed when I do ponder the weight of your reasons, I cannot deny, but these things are true. But whilst hazards and inconveniences do occur, which follow on the back of this opinion, my mind as it were tyed up with a Bridle, doth instantly I know not how, fail me, and bendeth from that too Stoical and severe right way towards utility, and almost falleth away. For if it shall be lawful for any Man to kill a Tyrant, see how great a gap you do open for wicked Men to commit any mischief, and how great hazard you create to good Men : to wicked Men you permit licentiousness, and lets out upon all the perturbation of all things. For he that shall kill a good King, or at least none of the worst, may he not pretend by his wicked

ed deed some shew of honest and lawful duty? or if any good Subject shall in vain attempt to kill a Prince worthy of all punishment, or accomplish what he intended to do, how great a confusion of all things do you suppose must needs follow thereupon? Whilst the wicked do tumultuate, raging that their head and leader is taken away from them; neither will all good men approve the deed, nor will all those who do approve the deed, defend the doer and Author of their liberty against a wicked crew. And many under an honest pretext of Peace will vail their own laziness, or rather caluminate the vertue of others, than confess their own slothfulness. surely this remembrance of self interest, and excuse of leaving the Publick cause and the fear of dangers, if it doth not break the Courage, yet it weakneth the same, and compelleth it to prefer tranquillity, albeit not very sure, to an uncertain expectation of liberty. *B.* If you will remember what is before spoken, this your fear will be easily discussed. For we told you that there be some Tyrannies allowed by the free suffrages of a People, which we do honour with Royal Titles, because of the moderate administration. No man, with my will, shall put violent hands on any such, nor yet on any of those, who even by force or fraud have acquitted soveraignty, provided they use a moderate way in their Government. Such amongst the *Remans* were *Vespasianus, Titus, Partinax*; *Alexander* amongst the *Grecians*, and *Hiero* in *Syracusa.* Who albeit they obtained the Government by Force and Arms, yet by their Justice and Equity deserved to be reckoned amongst just Kings. Besides, I do only shew what may be lawfully done, or ought to be done in this case, but do not exhort to attempt any such thing. For in the first a due consideration of the case, and a clear Explanation thereof is sufficient: but in the last there is need of good Counsel in undertaking, of Prudence in assaulting, and courage in acting. Now seeing these things are either promoted or overturned by the circumstances of Time, Person, Place, and other Instruments in carrying on the business: if any shall rashly attempt this, the blame of his fault can be no more imputed to me, than his fault to a Physitian, who hath duely described the Remedies of Diseases, but were given by another to the Patient unseasonably. *M.* One thing seems yet to be wanting to put an end to this dispute: which if you shall add, I shall think I have received a very singular kindness of you: the matter is this, let me understand, if there be any Church Censures against Tyrants? *B.* You may take it when you please out of the first Epistle of *Paul* to the *Corinthians,* where the Apostle doth forbid to have any Fellowship either at Meat or discourse with openly lewd and flagitious men. If this were observed amongst

Christians

Chriſtians, ſuch lewd Men, unleſs they did repent, might periſh by hunger, cold, and nakedneſs. *M.* A grievous ſentence indeed that is. But I do not know if a People, that allow ſo much liberty every way to their *Rulers,* will believe that Kings ſhould be puniſhed after this manner. *B.* Surely the Ancient Eccleſiaſtick Writers without Exceptions did thus underſtand that ſentence of *Paul.* For *Ambroſe* did hold out of the Aſſembly of the Chriſtians *Theodoſius the Emperour,* *Theodoſius* obeyed the ſaid Biſhop: and for what I know, Antiquity doth more highly extol the deed of no other ſo much, nor is the modeſty of any other Emperour more commended. But to our purpoſe, what difference is there betwixt the Excluſion out of Chriſtian fellowſhip, and the interdiction from Fire and Water? this laſt is a moſt grievous ſentence impoſed by *Rulers* againſt ſuch as refuſe to obey their Commands: and the former is a Sentence of Church-men. Now the puniſhment of the contempt of both Authorities is death: but the Secular Judge denounceth the death of the Body, the Eccleſiaſtick Judge denounceth the deſtruction of the whole Man. Therefore the Church will not account him worthy of death, whom it doth expel out of the fellowſhip of Chriſtians, while he is alive, and baniſheth him into the fellowſhip of Devils, when dead. Thus according to the equity of the cauſe I think I have ſpoken abundantly, if therewith any Forraigners be diſpleaſed, I deſire they would conſider how unjuſtly they deal with us. For whilſt there be many Nations both great and wealthy in *Europe,* having all their own peculiar Laws, they deal arrogantly who would preſcribe to all that Model and Form of Government which they themſelves enjoy. The *Helvetians* Government is a Common-wealth, *Germany* uſeth the name or Title of Empire, as a lawful Government. Some Cities in *Germany,* as I am (informed) are under the Rule of Princes, The *Venetians* have a Seniority tempered of theſe. *Muſcovia* hath a very Tyranny inſtead of Government. We have indeed but a little Kingdom, but we have enjoy'd it theſe two thouſand Years free of the Empire of forraign Nations. We did create at firſt lawful Kings, we did impoſe upon our ſelves and them equal and juſt Laws, the long continuance of time, doth ſhew they were uſeful. For more by the obſervation thereof than by force of Arms, hath this Kingdom ſtood intire hitherto: Now what iniquity is this, that we ſhould deſire either to abrogate, or neglect the Laws, the good whereof we have found by experience for ſo many Ages? Or what impudence is that in others, that whereas they cannot ſcarce defend their own Government, endeavour to weaken the ſtate and good order of another Kingdom? What? are not our Laws and Statues uſeful not only to our ſelves, but alſo

also to our Neighbours? For what can be more useful for keeping Peace with our nearest Neighbours, than the moderation of Kings? for from immoderate Lust unjust Wars are for the most part rashly undertaken, wickedly prosecuted and carried on, and shamefully with much disgrace left off. And further, what more hurtful can there be to any Common-wealth, than bad Laws amongst their nearest Neighbours, whereof the contagion doth usually spread far and wide? And why do they thus trouble us only, seeing so many Nations round about have their several Laws and Statutes of their own, and no Nation hath altogether the same Laws and Statutes as others about them have? and why are they now offended at us, seeing we make no new Law, but continue to observe what we had by an ancient Priviledge? and seeing we are not the only Persons, nor the first Persons, nor yet is it at this time that we make use of our Laws. But our Laws are displeasing to some. Perhaps their own Laws displease them also. We do not curiously enquire what the Laws of other Nations are. Let them leave us our own well known by the Experience of so many Years. Do we trouble their Councils? or in what business do we molest them? But you are seditious, say they. I could freely give them an Answer? what is that to them? we are tumultuous at our own peril, and our own damage. I might enumerate a great many seditions that are hurtful either to Common-wealths or Kingdoms, but I shall not make use of that defence. I deny any Nation to be less _____ than we. I deny that any Nation hath ever been more moderate in _____ than we. Many contentions have fallen out for Laws, and right of Goverment and administration of the Kingdom, yet the main business hath been still kept safe. Our contentions never were, as amongst many others, with the destruction of the People, nor with the hatred of our Princes, but only out of love to our own Country, and desire to maintain our Laws How often in our time have great Armies stood in opposition to one another? how oft have they retired and withdrawn from one another, not only without wound but without any harm, yea without so much as a reproach? How often hath the publick utility setled the private grudges? how often hath the rumour of the Enemies approach extinguished our intestine hatred and animosity? In all our Seditions we have not been more modest than fortunate; seeing for the most part the Party most just hath been always most fortunate: and even as we have moderately vented our hatred, so have we to our profit and advantage condescended to an agreement. These things at present do occur, which might seem to compesce the Speeches of Malevolents refute such as are more pertinatious, and may satisfie such as are of a more temperate disposition. But by what right other Nations are govern'd, I thought it not much to our purpose. I have briefly rehearsed our own way and custom, but yet more amply than I intended or than the matter did require: because I undertook this pains for you only. And if it be approved by you, I have enough. *M.* As for me, you have abundantly satisfied me: but if I can satifie others also, I shall think I have received much good by your discourse, and my self eased of very much trouble.

FINIS.

www.ingramcontent.com/pod-product-compliance
Lightning Source LLC
Chambersburg PA
CBHW020230090426
42735CB00010B/1633